BIG KNIT LOVE

20 CHUNKY KNIT FASHIONS

Linda Zemba Burhance

The Taunton Press

The Taunton Press
Inspiration for hands-on living®

The Taunton Press, Inc., 63 South Main Street,
PO Box 5506, Newtown, CT 06470-5506
Email:tp@taunton.com

Editor: April Mohr
Copy Editor: Betty Christiansen
Indexer: Cathy Goddard
Jacket/Cover Design: Kimberly Adis
Interior Design: Kimberly Adis
Layout: Kimberly Adis
Photographer: Helen Norman, except pp. 9–42, 50, 51, 55 (left), 60, 61, 63, 66, 71, 74, 78, 87, 97, 103, 105, 109, 115, 118, 119, 122, 123, 126, 127, 131, 134, 136, 137, 141, 142, 143 (left), 148, and 151 by Scott Phillips © The Taunton Press, Inc.

The following names/manufacturers appearing in *Big.Knit.Love.* are trademarks: Buttercream™ Luxe Craft, Isaac Mizrahi® Craft™ by Premier® Yarns, LB Collection®, Lion Brand®, Lion Brand Fun Fur®, Lion Brand Heartland® Thick & Quick®, Lion Brand Hometown USA®, Lion Brand Martha Stewart Crafts™/ᴹᶜ, Lion Brand Romance®, Lion Brand Tweed Stripes®, Lion Brand Wool-Ease® Thick & Quick®, Loops & Threads® Fabulous Fur™, Offray®, Patons® Cobbles™, Red Heart® Boutique Boulevard™, Red Heart Boutique Swanky™, Red Heart Grande™, Red Heart Grande Metallic™, Scotch®, Slinky®

Library of Congress Cataloging-in-Publication Data

Names: Burhance, Linda Zemba, author.
Title: Big knit love : 20 chunky knit fashions / Linda Zemba Burhance.
Description: Newtown, CT : Taunton Press, Inc., [2017] | Includes index.
Identifiers: LCCN 2016037032 | ISBN 9781631864513
Subjects: LCSH: Knitting--Patterns. | Knitwear.
Classification: LCC TT825 .B86545 2017 | DDC 746.43/2--dc23
LC record available at https://lccn.loc.gov/2016037032

Printed in the United States of America
10 9 8 7 6 5 4 3 2 1

DEDICATION

To my husband, Frank, for supporting my dreams
and to my son, Noah, for inspiring them.

BIG LOVE, LINDA

ACKNOWLEDGMENTS

I WOULD LIKE TO ACKNOWLEDGE THE FOLLOWING people at The Taunton Press for their incredible dedication to making this book possible.

Carolyn Mandarano, acquiring editor, for seeing the love in this book.

April Mohr, for her technical edits and all-around knitting knowledge. Thank you for your effort in making this book accurate for all the knitters who will read it.

Rosalind Loeb Wanke, book art director, for the dedication to making this an art piece as much as a knitting book.

I would also like to extend my gratitude to the following people for their extraordinary talent in contributing to the BIG look and feel of this book: Lynne Phillips, production manager; Betty Christiansen, copy editor; Kim Adis, cover and interior design; Helen Norman, photographer for beauty photos; Scott Phillips, photographer for process photos.

And finally, I would like to extend a warm word of appreciation to Karen Freeman and Red Heart brand yarn for their donations of Jumbo yarns and help with Jumbo labeling, and to Brandyce Pechillo and the marketing folks at Lion Brand Yarns for their continued support of my books. Thank you—I couldn't have done something this BIG without you!

CONTENTS

INTRODUCTION
BIG KNIT PROJECTS
USING CHUNKY YARNS AND BIG NEEDLES

I love "big" knitting because the texture drives me wild! It is fun and screams HANDMADE, and it's a much more exciting way to use your hands than working on a keyboard all day!

Chunky yarns and large-size needles make me happy. I cannot get enough of these bulky knits and the whimsical nature of the exaggerated-looking stitches they create. For me, the bigger the better. Knitting with these oversize needles and bulky yarns is relaxing and less structured than knitting with standard-size needles and yarns, which makes big knitting appealing to new and experienced knitters alike. Big knitting is fast and fashionable—what could be better than that? Fashionistas and knitting mavens are knitting up big knits over the weekend, so why not join the fun?

Many people are catching onto this oversize knits trend, and yarn companies are responding quite vigorously. The Craft Yarn Council (CYC) has recently added a whole new weight category of yarns: CYC 7 JUMBO. For those of you new to knitting, the CYC categorizes yarn thicknesses into a weight system, and understanding yarn weight classifications will help you choose the proper yarns for your projects. Up until now, the largest category was Super Bulky, or CYC 6.

The CYC number can be found on the paper wrapper around each skein of yarn and serves as a guide to help you choose the correct yarn for each project. As long as you choose yarn that has the same CYC number(s) as those listed in your pattern, you should be able to maintain the correct gauge. The gauge specifies the number of stitches and rows per inch that should be attained in the project and helps you achieve the correct finished measurements, giving you the same results as those shown in the pattern. With this information in hand, feel free to experiment and let your personality shine through in a BIG way!

If you are one of those people who loves to "knit big" or wants to learn how, please join me in my journey to show you some *BIG.KNIT.LOVE*. I begin with the basics: casting on, knit stitch, purl stitch, and casting off. I then take you through some of the standard increase and decrease stitch techniques used to provide shape or visual surface interest to the project. For example, a curved neckline and an angled shoulder utilize increase and decrease stitches to create their shape. I have also included several finishing details, such as connecting and seaming techniques, edging ideas, trims, pom-poms, and fringe.

CREATIVE KNITTERS ARE MAKING BIG KNITS
out of giant strands and roving yarns, and others are making super-large needles from plastic tubing and wood.

Each project highlights a different technique or style idea—but there's more! If you have read any of my previous books, you will see a common thread, and that is the technique of multistrand knitting. Multistrand knitting will enable you to achieve a big knit look by grouping various combinations of yarn types and weights, holding them together, and treating them as one while you knit. I love this technique because it is a fantastic way to demonstrate your own aesthetic preferences.

Although I have given you suggested yarns and colors, you should feel free to come up with your own yarn and color combinations using the CYC numbers listed in the pattern. Remember, the CYC number is a guide, so be sure to create a gauge swatch to see if your yarn combination achieves the required yarn bulk. Correct gauge isn't as important in scarves and other projects that don't require exact fit. But when making a sweater or other fitted or sculpted item, it is essential to achieve proper gauge. (Gauge is discussed in more detail on p. 42.)

I have enjoyed seeing the big knit trend evolve. Creative knitters are making big knits out of giant strands and roving yarns, and others are making super-large needles from plastic tubing and wood. I recently purchased some handmade, super-giant needles (3 ft. tall,

size 150) to experiment with. Now those are some big needles!

I have even attended a local library info and training session to try my hand at 3D printing some super-chunky needles (I estimate them to be size 70). Come to find out, there are others like me who have already created the 3D printer files and made them available online . . . who knew? Maybe you should check out your local library to see if the appropriate technology is available to help you print some big needles. Have fun experimenting. I know I am having a blast exploring this idea and my passion for knitting.

Whatever your passion in life, big or small, I wish you the best and commend you for following your heart. My heart and soul went into the making of *BIG.KNIT.LOVE.*, so I hope you enjoy it!

Linda

THE
BASICS

KNITTING BIG BASICS

Chunky yarns amp up the volume! Whether you're a beginner just learning to knit or a seasoned knitter who wants to knit up a project quickly, these yarns are beautiful, are easy to work with, and knit up into stylish projects in no time. Big yarns work up quickly to produce knitted pieces that have a rich texture and definition. The oversize stitches produced with big yarns certainly make a bold statement about personal style. Beginners especially will love knitting with these yarns since the stitches are easy to see.

Chunky yarns and the needles used to work with them may appear larger than life, but other than that, pattern instructions are the same as for other knitted patterns.

This section includes techniques and other information every knitter should know before starting any knitting project—BIG or small!

BASIC NEEDLE SIZES

This book has been written to account for the big, bigger, and biggest needles available on the market. Sizes 17, 19, 35, 36, and 50 are used in various projects, and all tools are listed in the materials section.

Of course, the experienced knitter knows that needles can be straight, circular, or double-pointed. But if you're a beginner, you should know why there are different types. Straight needles are the most commonly used for knitting,

and they come in a variety of materials, such as wood, metal, or plastic. Most people choose their favorites by the way the needles feel when they are knitting with them. Plastic tends to have more give in your hands, wood tends to keep the yarn on the needle and is a green approach, and metal tends to allow the knitting to slide very easily—the hollow versions are super-lightweight. I suggest you buy a few different types to see what you like best.

Circular needles are mainly used to knit something "in the round," like a cowl; however, they are extremely useful for large projects that are heavy or have a lot of stitches. In those cases, the needles can be used as if they are straight needles. You work the project back and forth, and the weight of the project is distributed on the cable of the needle as you knit.

Double-pointed needles are typically used in sets of four or five to knit smaller circles in the round. I don't use them in this book, but they are an option for the experienced knitter.

There are also a few artisanal needles on the market, handcrafted for the knitting community by dedicated artists. I designed the garments in this book based on the needle sizes that are most commonly available, but I encourage you to experiment with as many options as you can find.

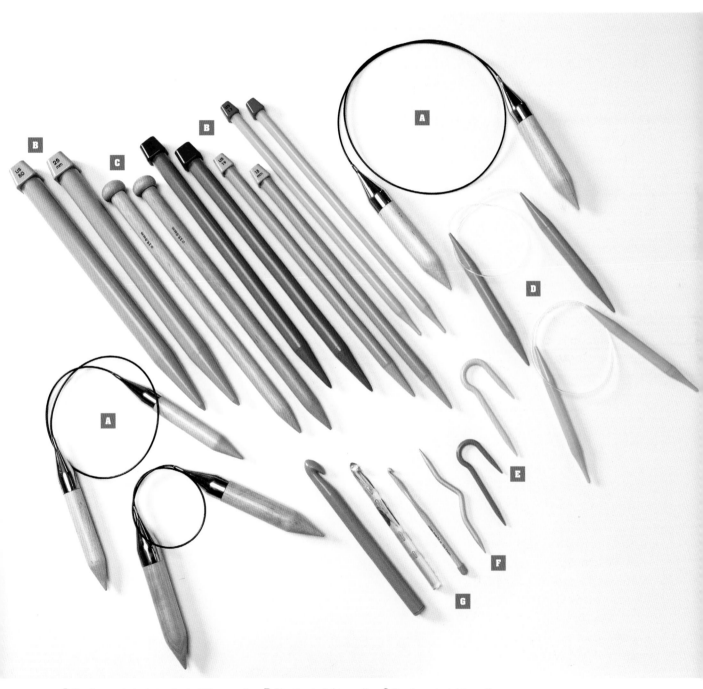

A Bamboo and steel circular knitting needles **B** Plastic straight needles **C** Bamboo straight needles
D Plastic circular knitting needles **E** Cable hooks **F** Cable needle **G** Metal and plastic crochet hooks

YARN SIZES/WEIGHTS

Most of the patterns require yarn that falls into three standard size categories:

- Category 5: Bulky
- Category 6: Super Bulky
- Category 7: Jumbo

Category 7 (Jumbo) is a new yarn weight category created by the Craft Yarn Council, which is one of the most exciting events to happen to BIG knitters! We now have our own category, and because of that, more bulky yarn varieties are being created by yarn manufacturers.

In case you can't find Jumbo yarns in your area, I have included several patterns that use multiple yarn strands held together and worked as one to simulate the category 6 and 7 yarns worked with the biggest needles. Experiment with your own choices. It is a great way to explore your inner designer and a fantastic yarn "stash buster" exercise.

Yarn, regardless of size, is sold in balls, skeins, or hanks. Balls look like you would expect a ball to look; skeins are more tubular and usually contain more yarn than found in a ball; a hank is typically how a roving or hand-spun yarn is sold, in a loosely wound and twisted circle. Although they mean different things, these words are sometimes used interchangeably.

Whatever type of knitting you enjoy, I hope you have fun doing it. Knitting and I are BFFs (Big Fashion Friends), and I would love to see you foster your own BIG ideas!

STANDARD
YARN WEIGHT SYSTEM

Recently, the Craft Yarn Council added a seventh category to its Yarn Weight System called Jumbo in recognition of the variety of super-thick yarns that have been introduced in the market. This addition also resulted in slight gauge adjustments to its Super Bulky category 6. According to the Craft Yarn Council website, the goal with this change is to make it easier for crocheters and knitters to understand the type of fabric these Jumbo yarns create and the range of hooks and needles generally required.

See the crochet and knit gauge ranges in the chart at right for the new Jumbo Yarn Weight category 7 and also note the slight gauge change for Super Bulky Yarn Weight category 6. The chart also provides recommendations for needle size and gauge based on the category of yarn.

This chart is based on 1 strand of yarn knit in stockinette stitch. In this book, sometimes multiple strands are used together, therefore allowing the needle size to be bigger. Follow the pattern instructions for the best results.

YARN WEIGHT SYMBOL & CATEGORY NAMES	5 BULKY	6 SUPER BULKY	7 JUMBO
TYPE OF YARNS IN CATEGORY	Chunky, Craft, Rug	Super Bulky, Roving	Jumbo, Roving
KNIT GAUGE RANGE IN STOCKINETTE STITCH TO 4 IN.	12–15 sts	7–11 sts	6 sts & fewer
RECOMMENDED NEEDLE IN METRIC SIZE RANGE	5.5–8 mm	8–12.75 mm	12.75 mm & larger
RECOMMENDED NEEDLE IN U.S. SIZE RANGE	9–11	11–17	17 & larger
CROCHET GAUGE RANGES IN SINGLE CROCHET TO 4 IN.	8–11 sts	7–9 sts	6 sts & fewer
RECOMMENDED HOOK IN METRIC SIZE	6.5–9 mm	9–15 mm	15 mm & larger
RECOMMENDED HOOK IN U.S. SIZE RANGE	K-10½ – M-13	M-13-Q	Q & larger

BASIC KNITTING SUPPLIES

Have these items on hand (as shown in the photo on p. 9 and the photo on the facing page), and you can make any of the projects in this book.

- Knitting needles (sizes are listed with the instructions for each project; **A**, **B**, **C**, and **D** in the photo on p. 9)

- Stitch holders in various sizes (**F** in the photo on the facing page)

- Cable hook or cable needle (**E** and **F** in the photo on p. 9), needed for creating cables used in patterns that include the Cable Stitch (although a large crochet hook can also be used)

- Stitch markers, which can be made of wood, plastic, or yarn scraps (**D**, **E**, and **G** in the photo on the facing page). These are used to mark a particular area of knitting that you have to keep track of, such as an increase or decrease in the work, or a change of pattern. You'll find various types of stitch markers on the market, but be sure they will fit your large needles before purchasing them. To make the yarn scrap version, simply wrap a short piece of contrasting yarn around the needle and tie a knot, creating a loop that fits exactly around the needle; trim the yarn ends.

- Crochet hook (**G** in the photo on p. 9) for connecting knitted pieces together or as a Jumbo cabling tool alternative

- Scissors (**B** in the photo on the facing page)

- Pom-pom maker (**A** in the photo on the facing page) for certain projects. You can always make a pom-pom by wrapping yarn around a piece of cardboard and cutting the yarn into a neat little stack (see pp. 142–143), but there are some great pom-pom makers on the market that are fun and easy to use. I recommend using heavy-duty sewing thread rather than yarn to gather the yarn pieces together in the pom-pom's center. You will be able to pull the center very tightly, keeping the pom-pom stable and preventing the strands of yarn from working their way out of the finished pom-pom.

- Rotary cutter and self-repairing cutting mat for cutting fringe (optional)

- Gauge ruler or straightedge ruler (**C** in the photo on the facing page)

- Sewing needle and matching thread. Not all projects require a needle and thread, but projects created with a loose knit and those that are knitted in Jumbo yarn will, for securing the yarn ends.

- Chip clips without teeth (**H** in the photo on the facing page). I like the kind typically used to close a bag of chips or other snacks.

A Pom-pom maker **B** Scissors **C** Ruler for measuring gauge **D** Jumbo wooden stitch markers
E Yarn scrap stitch markers **F** Stitch holders **G** Plastic stitch markers **H** Chip clips without teeth

BASIC STITCHES

Basic knitting stitches are important to know regardless of what size yarn or needles you're working with. As you read the pattern instructions, refer to the techniques below to help ensure success when knitting.

Long-Tail Cast-On

The Long-Tail Cast-On is a method used to put the first row of stitches onto the needle that creates a beautiful and consistent knitted edge. There are many cast-on methods, but this particular method is vitally important for big knits to stabilize the edge and prevent overstretching. It is also the method that visually looks most like a cast-off edge (the final row of stitches in a knitted piece), so if both ends of your scarf are hanging down side by side, they look even and consistent. The Long-Tail Cast-On consists of first making a slip knot, then adding (by casting on) the number of stitches required in the pattern instructions as shown in the steps below.

STEP 1: MAKE A SLIP KNOT

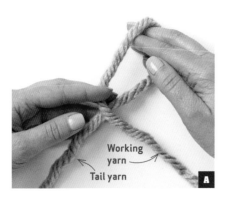 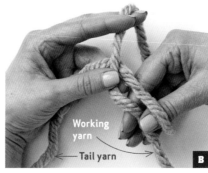 

Measure off at least a yard (or the length indicated in the pattern) of yarn or yarns (if you're using more than one yarn and treating them as one). Without cutting the yarn, cross the tail yarn under the working yarn to make a loop (photo **A**).

The working yarn is the yarn that is connected to your skein or ball of yarn. The tail yarn is the yarn that ends a few inches, feet, or yards from the needle.

Insert your hand into the loop and grab the working yarn (photo **B**).

Pull the working yarn through the loop, creating a new loop called the slip knot (photo **C**).

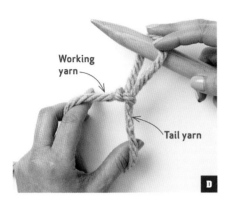

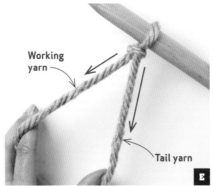

Place the slip knot on your knitting needle with the tail yarn on the front side of the needle as shown in photo **D**, and snug the knot to the needle by gently pulling on the working and tail yarns (photo **E**).

Pulling the working yarn will tighten the loop around the needle, and pulling the tail yarn will tighten the knot at the base of the loop. It might take some practice, but you want to make the slip knot snug enough to close any gaps around the needle yet loose enough to slide easily along the needle. The slip knot counts as one of your cast-on stitches.

A WORD ABOUT
KNITTING STYLES & METHODS

There are several knitting styles—continental, English, and American, among others. I am a continental knitter, so my working yarn is always on the hand opposite the working needle. (I'm right-handed, so I hold the working needle in my right hand and the yarn in my left hand, and all photos will reflect that. Some continental lefties work opposite to this.) I find the continental knitting style to be beneficial in several ways. I have more consistent and even tension because I am moving the working needle to grasp the yarn and don't have to stop and "let go" of the yarn in order to place the yarn over the needle. I am using both hands to knit, so there is less fatigue. I can "feel" the knitting with both hands, so there are fewer opportunities to pull the stitches too tightly.

There are many other styles of knitting, and regardless of which you choose, the working needle refers to the needle where new stitches are formed. The nonworking needle refers to the needle holding the stitches from the previously stitched row or the cast-on row. It's an odd (but standard) knitting term, because both needles are almost always working!

If you are constantly struggling with stitches that are too tight, why not try the continental method? If you are left-handed, you also may find this method preferable. There is no right or wrong method; it's a matter of preference. The point is to explore knitting styles and techniques until knitting becomes fun and stress-free. Knitting should reduce stress, not the other way around!

STEP 2: CAST ON STITCHES

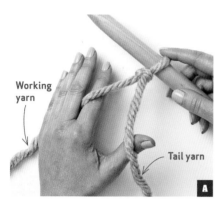

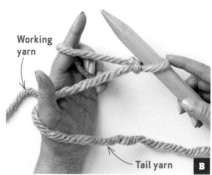

While holding the knitting needle in your right hand (place your right pointer finger on the slip knot to prevent it from accidentally sliding off the needle), create a Y with the hanging yarns by placing your left thumb and pointer finger between the tail and working yarns. The tail yarn should be over your thumb, and the working yarn should be over your pointer finger, as shown in photo **A**.

Pull back your left hand so your palm shows, and spread your thumb and pointer fingers apart (photo **B**); secure the ends of the tail and working yarns with your pinkie and ring finger.

Now slide the needle's point under the tail yarn on the left side of your thumb from left to right (photo **C**)...

...and over the working yarn on the left side of your pointer finger from right to left (photo **D**).

Pull the needle toward your body and through the loop created between the yarns on your thumb from right to left (photo **E**).

Release your thumb from the newly formed stitch (photo **F**).

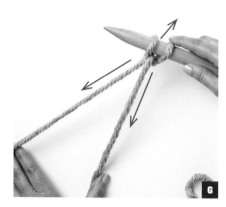

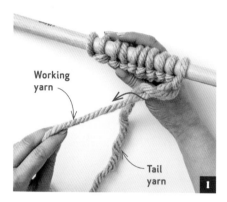

Gently pull the working and tail yarns to snug the stitch on the needle (photo **G**). Once again, pulling the working yarn will tighten the loop around the needle; pulling the tail yarn will tighten the knot at the bottom of the new stitch. As with the slip knot, you want the cast-on stitch to be snug enough to close any gaps but loose enough to slide along the needle.

Continue following the instructions for casting on until you have as many stitches on your needle as the pattern requires (counting the slip knot as the first stitch). Just be sure that your work stays straight along the bottom edge of the needle (the knotted parts of the stitches) and doesn't twist around the needle as you are adding stitches (photo **H**).

When I am about to begin to knit the first row after the cast-on, I take the extra step of twisting the tail yarn around the working yarn (photo **I**). It makes a nice corner and helps keep the work snug on the first row.

Loop Cast-On

An alternative method of casting on, called the Loop Cast-On, is a method needed in certain patterns. When required, this method will be noted.

Start with a slip knot as described on pp. 14–15. Then, holding the needle in your right hand, create a loop around your pointer finger with the tail end over the working end (photo **A**).

Slide the needle point into the loop from the top (photo **B**).

Snug the stitch close to the adjacent stitches (photo **C**).

Add additional loops as required (photo **D**).

The Loop Cast-On is also used when you want to add extra stitches at the end of a row in a work already in progress, but in that case you will not need to start with a slip knot; you just add the loops specified in the pattern as shown in photos **B**, **C**, and **D**.

WHAT IS A KNIT STITCH?

The word *knit* can be confusing to new knitters because it has more than one definition. It is used to describe a completed project made on knitting needles (a knit scarf, a knit hat, etc.) or the process of creating such a project (I just knitted a hat). The project might incorporate many types of stitches, including knit, purl, cables, increases, decreases, or other stitch combinations.

The word *knit* also refers to a specific stitch called the knit stitch. The usage of the word determines its definition. A knit stitch is usually considered to be the most basic stitch, and you can make an entire project using only this one stitch. When you do, the pattern is called Garter Stitch, but more on that later.

A knit stitch is shown above, and it is usually found on the front (also called face, right side, or outside) of the finished work. Notice the columns of V's created by the knit stitch.

Knit Stitch

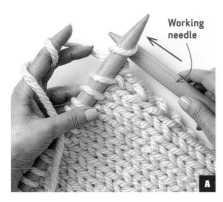

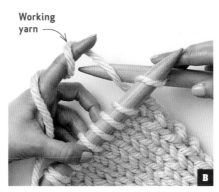

Place the needle with either your cast-on stitches or work in progress in your left hand. With the working needle in your right hand, and the yarn behind the work, insert the point into the front of the first stitch from left to right, and move the working needle behind the nonworking needle so that they are crossed (photo **A**).

Lift the working yarn and place it over the working needle so that the yarn wraps up and over the working needle, as shown in photo **B**. This will become your new stitch. Be sure your stitch looks like this. If it is the opposite of what is shown, you've made a whole different type of stitch. Keep trying until you get it.

Next, pull the new stitch through the old stitch by bringing the needle toward your body, gently releasing the working yarn over the tension finger on your opposite hand (left hand in the photo) to adjust the new stitch's tightness (photo **C**).

Slide the old stitch off the nonworking needle as you pull the new stitch through. The first new stitch has been formed on the working needle (photo **D**).

Repeat this process for additional knit stitches (photo **E**). When you complete a row, you'll switch needles so that the working needle becomes the nonworking needle and the nonworking needle becomes the working needle ready to create another new row.

Purl Stitch

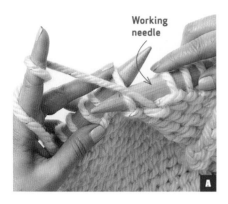

Working needle

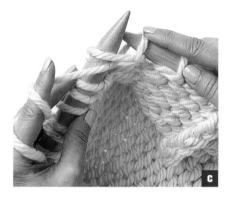

Move the working yarn to the front of the working needle. Place the working needle into the front of the first stitch from right to left so that the working needle crosses in front of the nonworking needle and the tips point in opposite directions (photo **A**).

NOTE: The working needle is on the right in the photo. It's where all new stitches are formed.

Wrap the working yarn up and over the top of the working needle (photo **B**).

Pull the yarn through the old stitch from left to right to create a new stitch on the working needle (photo **C**).

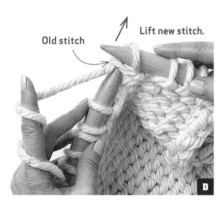

Old stitch

Lift new stitch.

New stitch

Remove the old stitch from the nonworking needle as you pull the new stitch through (photo **D**). The arrow points to the newly formed purl stitch (photo **E**).

Repeat this process for additional purl stitches if the pattern calls for them (photo **F**). Remember to put the yarn to the front before beginning the next purl stitch.

When you complete a row, you'll switch needles so that the working needle becomes the nonworking needle and vice versa.

Casting Off

Sometimes referred to as "binding off," casting off is how you remove stitches from the needles, closing or ending the work while preventing the knitted piece from unraveling.

First stitch

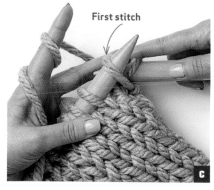
First stitch

Begin a cast-off by knitting a sequence of 2 stitches (photo **A**).

Cross the nonworking needle in front of the working needle and insert it into the first stitch in the sequence as shown in photos **B** and **C**.

Continued

THE BASIC STITCHES: KNIT & PURL

The two primary stitches in knitting are knit and purl. The two stitches are complete opposites. A knit stitch looks like a purl stitch on the opposite side of your work, and vice versa. This characteristic is helpful when creating any project. If you want the outside (or front of the work) to look like knit stitches throughout, you would use the knit stitch when working on the outside and the purl stitch when working on the inside (or back of the work). Purl stitches look like knit stitches on the reverse side. Using this technique (knitting all outside rows and purling all inside rows) is known as the Stockinette Stitch.

Stockinette Stitch, knit side

Stockinette Stitch, purl side

Continued from p. 21

Lift the first stitch up and over the second stitch, and pass the first stitch off the needle (photo **D**).

One stitch remains (photo **E**). You have reduced the total number of stitches by 1.

If additional cast-off stitches are required in the pattern instructions, knit another stitch so that once again there are 2 stitches on the working needle.

Repeat this process as many times as needed across the row, following the pattern instructions for the project (photo **F**).

If you are casting off the entire row of stitches, repeat this process until only 1 stitch remains on the working needle and all other stitches have been removed from the nonworking needle.

Pull tail yarn through.

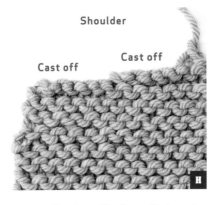

Shoulder

Cast off

Cast off

Simply cut the yarn at least 6 in. from the needle, or as indicated in your pattern, and pull this tail through the last stitch to complete the cast-off row (photo **G**).

NOTE: Casting off a few stitches at the beginning or end of every other row, rather than the entire row, can be used for shaping the work, such as in an underarm, neckline, or shoulder (photo **H**).

When most patterns indicate it is time to cast off, it is usually while knitting, as shown on p. 21. However, casting off can be done while purling as well, or with other stitch combinations. The same process as outlined on p. 21 is used. Work 2 stitches in the sequence; then lift the first stitch over the second and drop it off the needle as shown on p. 21. Be sure to read all patterns thoroughly for these unique instances. If the pattern doesn't indicate which stitch combination(s) to use in a cast-off row, use the knit stitch.

COMMONLY USED STITCH COMBINATIONS: GARTER STITCH, STOCKINETTE STITCH, AND RIB STITCH

Now that you have mastered the knit stitch and the purl stitch, you can begin learning how to combine the stitches to make various stitch combinations.

Garter Stitch

When you KNIT every row across the FRONT and the BACK of the work, you create the Garter Stitch (shown at left, top). It looks similar to the purl side of Stockinette Stitch (described below), but there is a larger space between the purl rows where the knit rows "reside." This look can also be achieved by purling every row; however, it will be referred to as Reverse Garter Stitch. It is sometimes needed in patterns depending on the position of the work.

Front of work, knit side

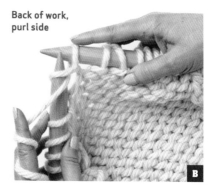

Back of work, purl side

Stockinette Stitch

Stockinette Stitch is made by using a knit stitch for every stitch on every row on the FRONT of the work (photo **A**) and a purl stitch for every stitch on every row on the BACK of the work (photo **B**). This is what the work looks like when you are creating the Stockinette Stitch.

Rib Stitch

A Rib Stitch is formed when you alternate a knit stitch and a purl stitch across each row (photos **A** and **B**).

A Knit 1, Purl 1 (abbreviated K1, P1) pattern worked across a row is commonly referred to as a 1 x 1 (one-by-one) Rib Stitch. A Rib Stitch is normally done in areas where extra stretch is needed, such as cuffs or hems, but an entire garment can be made out of Rib Stitch and usually results in a garment that hugs the body's contours. A 1 x 1 Rib Stitch looks similar to the knit side of Stockinette Stitch, but there is a larger space between the columns of knit stitches where the purl stitches "reside." An example of a 1 x 1 Rib Stitch is shown stretched in photo B, where you can more clearly see the purl stitches between the knit stitches. When doing

any Rib Stitch combination, you must begin each knit stitch with the yarn behind the work and every purl stitch with the yarn in front of the work. That means the yarn needs to be moved each time you switch from knit to purl and vice versa.

You can also do a Knit 2, Purl 2 (K2, P2) pattern to create a wider-looking rib, or 2 x 2 (two-by-two) Rib Stitch.

Rib Stitches can be made using an even number of stitches across the row or an odd number of stitches across the row. The patterns in this book will indicate how to line up your ribbing correctly based on an odd or even number of stitches. Just follow the instructions and be sure to move the yarn from back to front or vice versa when you switch between knit and purl stitches!

KNIT, PURL & RIB STITCHES

When switching back and forth from knit stitches to purl stitches, be sure to move the yarn first. The yarn must be at the back of the work before you create a knit stitch, and it must be in the front of the work before you begin a purl stitch. Normally after you complete a knit stitch, the yarn is at the back, and when you complete a purl stitch, the yarn is in the front. When doing a Rib Stitch, you will have to remember to move the yarn from front to back or back to front before switching stitches from knit to purl or purl to knit. If you forget to move the yarn, you will end up with extra stitches in your row!

DECREASING AND INCREASING STITCHES

Decreases can create decorative knitting. Without decreasing (and increasing) stitches, your work would always be flat and rectangular—like a scarf or blanket. To give your work shape (for sweaters and other projects), you also need to incorporate decrease and increase stitches in your work. There are several to choose from, and each has specific visual characteristics. The pattern instructions will tell you when to use them. Here are descriptions of the decreasing and increasing stitches used in this book.

Decreasing Stitches

K2TOG: KNIT TWO TOGETHER

Knitting 2 stitches together (abbreviated as K2TOG) leaves 1 less stitch on the needle and is also used to create an angle or visible style line in the work.

Place the working needle through the front of 2 stitches as if they were 1 stitch (photo **A**).

NOTE: The front of a stitch is the part of the stitch on the needle that is visible as you look at the needle. The back of a stitch is the part of the stitch that appears behind the needle.

Next, create a new knit stitch by wrapping the working yarn up and over the working needle as shown in photo **B**.

Pull the new stitch through both old stitches as shown in photo **C**. Then lift the working needle as shown in photo **D** to begin sliding the old stitches up the nonworking needle.

Slide the 2 old stitches off the non-working needle as shown in photo **E**.

You can also do this type of decrease while purling (known as P2TOG or Purl Two Together). In the same manner, simply purl 2 stitches together, treating them as 1 stitch.

SSK: SLIP, SLIP, KNIT

This is another technique for knitting 2 stitches together at the same time. Like K2TOG, SSK is used to decrease the number of working stitches and/or create an angle or visible style line in the work. SSK creates an angle similar to a keyboard's back slash, but it is a mirror image of K2TOG, which creates an angle similar to a keyboard's front (or common) slash.

To SSK, slip 2 stitches knitwise one at a time onto the working needle without knitting them. *Knitwise* is a term used to describe how to move your stitch from one needle to the other. Knitwise means you place the working needle into the next stitch as if you're about to knit it (photo **A**).

To slip it, just slide the stitch to the working needle without creating a new stitch (photo **B**). (In other knit stitches, you may be asked to slip purlwise, meaning you insert the needle as if you're about to purl the stitch before you slip it.)

Then place the nonworking needle through the fronts of both slipped stitches on the working needle from left to right as shown in photo **C**. Notice that your needles are now in the correct position to create a knit stitch on the working needle, and that's exactly what you'll do!

Create your knit stitch by wrapping the working yarn up and over the working needle as shown in photo **D**.

Pull the yarn through the back of both stitches from left to right as shown in photo **E** and remove the slipped stitches from the nonworking needle as shown in photo **F**. This decrease can also be done with purl stitches, and, as you might guess, it is known as Slip, Slip, Purl or SSP.

Photo **G** shows examples of the style lines created by Slip, Slip, Knit (SSK) on the right and Knit Two Together (K2TOG) on the left. These two decreases are often used on opposite ends of the same knitted piece to give the piece style symmetry (see the photo on p. 98).

SKP: SLIP, KNIT, PASS

This is another technique to reduce the number of stitches on the needle and/or create an angle in the work, but it is not a mirror image of K2TOG. It produces more of a bump than an angle, so it is used for specific areas only, such shoulders, where the bump will not be obvious (photo **A**).

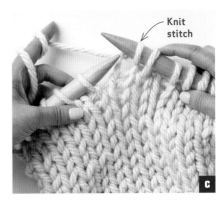

I am showing this SKP in the middle of the work because sometimes it will be used to decrease a neckline. Most often you will find decreases in underarms and shoulders, but decreases can create interesting shapes in the work as well.

To SKP, slip 1 stitch without knitting or purling it onto the working needle as shown in photo **B**. Slip it knitwise, meaning put the working needle into the stitch as if you're about to knit it, but simply slide it onto the working needle.

Knit the next stitch, removing the old stitch from the nonworking needle as shown in photo **C**.

Continued

Continued from p. 27

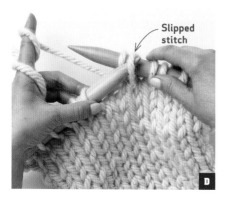

Using the nonworking needle, lift the slipped stitch up and pass it over the knitted stitch and off the working needle as shown in photos **D**, **E**, and **F**. One decrease is made.

SPP: SLIP, PURL, PASS

This is another technique to reduce the number of stitches on the needle and/or create an angle in the work when you are working on the purl side. To SPP, slip 1 stitch purlwise (as if to purl) onto the working needle without purling it. Purl the next stitch, then lift the slipped stitch up and over the purled stitch and pass it off the needle.

Increasing Stitches

There are many ways to increase the number of stitches in a row. The one that I use in this book is called Make One Front and Back (M1FB), also known as Knit One Front and Back (K1FB).

Photo **A** shows an example of M1FB at the beginning of the row. This will angle the work outward to the right.

M1FB: MAKE ONE FRONT AND BACK

Similar to some of the decrease stitches described previously, M1FB increases the number of working stitches, but it is also used to create an angle or visible style line in your work (photo **A**). You can make 1 stitch anywhere on the row, but here is how to make 1 stitch at the beginning of the row.

To M1FB at the beginning of the row, knit 1 stitch, but do not remove the old stitch from the nonworking needle (photos **B** and **C**).

Re-insert the working needle, this time into the back of the old stitch on the nonworking needle from right to left (photo **D**).

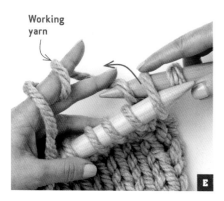

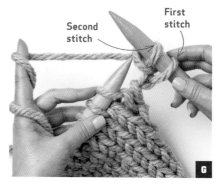

Complete the increase by wrapping the working yarn over the working needle (photo **E**).

Pull the working yarn through the back of the old stitch (photo **F**) to create an additional new stitch.

Remove the old stitch from the nonworking needle (photo **G**). You have created 2 stitches from 1 stitch by Making One in the Front and Back (M1FB) at the beginning of the row. Remember, this stitch can also be done in the middle or end of a row as directed by your pattern.

Picking Up Stitches

This technique is typically used when adding a new section or other feature, such as a collar, to a knitted piece that has already been bound off and removed from the needle. You actually create stitches from the finished edge to begin the new feature.

Insert your needle into an area of the finished work as specified by the pattern instructions (photo **A**).

Wrap the yarn around the needle (photo **B**) and pull it through the work to create the new stitch (photo **C**), trying to keep the tension even as you go.

Repeat as necessary until you have the desired number of picked-up stitches (photo **D**). It is helpful to count the number of spaces or rows first and divide the number of picked-up stitches required evenly across the desired section.

KNITTING IN THE ROUND

Some patterns in this book call for the use of circular needles and will instruct you to knit in the round. When you work with straight needles, you work back and forth across the needles, but when using circular needles, you most commonly just continue to work around and around. You can also use circular needles to knit back and forth, such as in a project where the work will be very heavy or too large for standard-length straight needles.

When knitting in the round, the first stitch that you knit on the first row will end up touching the last stitch on that same row, once you form it into a circle. Then, you will continue to knit around and around almost like a Slinky®. Knitting in the round is so much fun, but there is one very important detail to note as you begin.

When you connect your work in the round, take the time to look at your cast-on stitches. Make sure the knotted part of every single stitch is positioned downward along the bottom edge of the needle and none of the stitches are twisted around the needle (photos **A** and **B**). You don't want to have to rip out stitches.

Stitch markers are necessary to mark the end of the row while knitting in the round. With these big needles, I find it helpful to use a knotted piece of contrasting yarn to make my markers. It can be thinner yarn than the project yarn, but it shouldn't be thicker. I make a loop, tie it off, trim the tied ends, then slip the loop over the needle where a marker is needed.

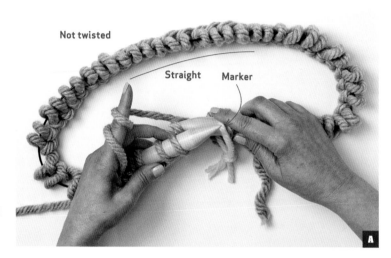

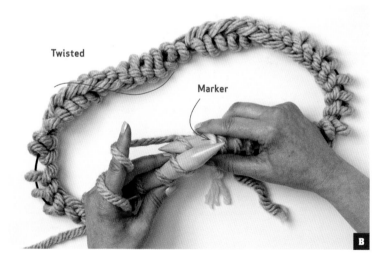

CABLES

Cables are the quintessential decorative stitch in knitting and can be approached in myriad ways. The patterns in this book will require you to either cable forward (CF) or cable back (CB), and the instructions will indicate a specific number in between the CF or CB abbreviations. The number designates the TOTAL number of stitches needed to make the cable.

In photo **A**, you can see that the cable is 6 stitches wide; therefore, we are knitting a C6F cable, which is to say that there are a total of 6 stitches in the width of the cable. When the "cabling" row is stitched, we put 3 stitches to the front (F in the abbreviation) of the work, wait to knit them until the next 3 are complete, then return them back on the needle and continue to knit. This is how the cable's twist is created, and it's actually easier than you might think. On most of the cable's rows, you'll simply knit and/or purl as directed. The pattern will clearly indicate when it's time to create the "twist." Here are the steps for C6F for you to learn and practice:

A

B

C

As shown in photo **B**, you'll knit or purl across the row as directed until you reach the start of the 6 cable stitches. Slide the first 3 cable stitches from the nonworking needle to a crochet hook, cable needle, or cable hook, whichever you prefer, and hold the crochet hook with the unworked stitches in FRONT of the work. Pictured here is a jumbo crochet hook.

Start using the working needle to knit the next 3 cable stitches from the nonworking needle, as shown in photo **C**. Knit them in the normal fashion.

Slide the initial 3 stitches one at a time back onto the nonworking needle in order, taking care not to twist them when putting them back on (photo **D**).

Once all stitches are back on the nonworking needle, set the crochet hook aside, and knit the 3 remaining stitches to complete the C6F pattern as shown in photo **E**. Then continue to knit the rest of row as directed in the pattern.

As you might guess, to cable back, as in C6B, for example, instead of holding the first 3 stitches in front of the work as shown in photo B, you hold them at the BACK (B in the abbreviation) of the work (in back of the working needle, away from your body). Then complete the remaining steps as above. The resulting cable turns in the opposite direction.

There are many variations on this theme, and the pattern instructions will specifically direct you, but once you master these two motions, the sky is the limit for making cables!

CONNECTING PIECES TOGETHER

There are various methods for connecting pieces together. In this book, we will use the following three methods: weaving back and forth to connect, mock grafting, and overcast method. Slip Stitch is another method explained under the section "Crochet Stitches" on p. 37.

WEAVE BACK AND FORTH TO CONNECT

Place one piece on top of the other, right sides facing, and align the edges that are to be connected row by row. Starting with a yarn tail or separate piece of yarn, as per the pattern instructions, insert a crochet hook into a spot on each side of the pieces, making sure they are in the same row if possible. Wrap the yarn around the crochet hook (photo **A**) and pull it all the way through (photo **B**). Flip over the pieces.

Continuing with the yarn tail or separate piece of yarn, as per the pattern instructions, insert the crochet hook into a spot on each side of the pieces just above the spot you completed, making sure they are in the same row if possible. Wrap the yarn around the crochet hook and pull it all the way through (photo **C**). Flip over the pieces.

Continue with this process until the seam is complete, weaving in tails when finished to secure (see the right side of the work in photo **D**).

MOCK GRAFTING

This technique is achieved when you have two cast-off edges that need to align and look like continuous knitting. You are mocking the look of the knitting by weaving through the knit stitches to create a simulated knit stitch.

Place the two pieces next to each other, aligning the edges to be connected row by row. Insert a crochet hook as shown in photo **A**, wrapping the yarn or the tail around the hook and pulling the yarn or tail all the way through the stitch (photos **B** and **C**).

Alternate each side of the seam as shown in photos **D** and **E**.

OVERCAST METHOD

Overcast method is a very simple way of connecting two pieces of work together. I prefer to use this method to connect pieces with straight edges. The other benefit of this method is that it can be used decoratively, sometimes even with a contrast yarn.

To overcast with bulky or chunky yarn I prefer to use a crochet hook. I find it is less likely to "split" the yarn, but a very large yarn needle can also be used.

Place the crochet hook on an angle through two stitches as pictured (photo **A**) and pull the yarn completely through the stitch (photo **B**). Repeat until the seam is connected and tie off and weave in the ends (photo **C**).

CROCHET STITCHES

To help anchor the edge of a project, to add a decorative edge, or to connect two knitted pieces together, some patterns may require the use of a crochet hook and a particular crochet stitch.

CROCHETED SLIP STITCH

This is actually a simple crochet stitch called a Slip Stitch, but it looks like a chain of stitches and is identical in appearance to a knitted cast-off edge. Isn't that convenient? It can also be used to connect two pieces of a garment together as mentioned previously, and it works really well for connecting straight edges, such as two side seams.

Any pattern in the book using this method will list the required crochet hook size. The one pictured here is U.S. size N or 15 (10 mm), and in this demonstration, I am duplicating the look of the cast-off edge on the right of the swatch with a contrasting blue yarn on the left of the swatch by slip-stitching into the cast-on edge, as shown in photo **A** on the facing page.

STEP 1: To make a crocheted Slip Stitch, start with a slip knot as shown on pp. 14–15, and place it on your crochet hook. For the first Slip Stitch in the row, place the crochet hook into a knitted cast-on stitch and wrap the yarn around the crochet hook. Pull the yarn back through the knitted stitch and then through the slip knot. One loop remains on the crochet hook (photo **A**).

STEP 2: Keep the loop on the crochet hook; then place the crochet hook into the next knitted cast-on stitch. Wrap the yarn around the crochet hook and pull the yarn through both the knitted stitch and the loop created in step 1 (photo **B**). A new loop remains on your crochet hook (photo **C**).

STEP 3: Repeat step 2 along the knitted edge as many times as required in your pattern instructions.

STEP 4: Cut the yarn, leaving at least a 6-in. tail, and pull it through the last stitch. Weave in the end. Trim the excess.

Loop on crochet hook, with slipped stitches on cast-on edge

Loop on crochet hook, with working yarn wrapped around crochet hook

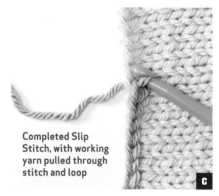

Completed Slip Stitch, with working yarn pulled through stitch and loop

SLIP STITCH FOLLOWED BY A CHAIN ONE EDGE

To help anchor the edge of a project, to add a decorative edge, or to connect two pieces together, some patterns may require a Slip Stitch followed by a Chain One combination to complete the edge. It produces an edge similar to a Slip Stitch, but it is more effective when the knitted stitches are a large distance apart (as when using big yarns!), especially when a thinner yarn is used to crochet the edge. It does end up having a slight wave to the edge, as shown in photo **A**.

To make a Slip Stitch Chain One edge, you will need a crochet hook. Any pattern in the book using this method will list the required crochet hook size. The one shown here is U.S. size N or 15 (10 mm). A review of the Slip Stitch, on p. 37, will be helpful in learning this more detailed edging, because you will alternate a Slip Stitch with a Chain One, but the instructions for both are provided here.

NOTE: The photo above shows a work in progress. To begin, always start with a slip knot as shown on pp. 14–15. Place the slip knot onto the crochet hook and into the work, and make one Slip Stitch to anchor the edge, following the steps on the facing page.

BEGIN SLIP STITCH, CHAIN ONE EDGE

Slip stitch chain one edge

A

Hook shown through stitch of knitted piece. Working yarn shown wrapped around hook.

B

C

Place the crochet hook into the knitted stitch. This is the first step to make the Slip Stitch. Wrap the working yarn around the crochet hook (photo **A**).

Then pull the yarn through the work and through the stitch on the knitted piece (photo **B**). You now have one loop on the hook.

The Slip Stitch is complete (photo **C**).

D

E

Continue in this manner, alternating the Slip Stitch with the Chain Stitch across the edge as instructed in the pattern. Once the pattern is complete, cut the yarn, leaving at least a 6-in. tail, and pull the yarn through the last stitch. Weave in the end. Trim the excess.

Next, without putting the hook into the work, wrap the yarn around the crochet hook and pull it through the loop on the hook (photo **D**).

A new loop is on the crochet hook (photo **E**). In crochet, this is called a Chain Stitch.

SINGLE CROCHET AND CHAIN STITCH EDGE

I have been known to break the rules sometimes, so I have created a signature edge method because of the bulk of the larger yarns and the desire to have a flat chain on the edge of the garment. I used a decorative sequined yarn here and alternated a Single Crochet and a Chain Stitch along the edge. You will notice the edge is much flatter than the Slip Stitch Chain One edge, but it does fan out slightly.

NOTE: The photo above shows a work in progress. To begin, always start with a slip knot as shown on pp. 14–15. Place the slip knot onto the crochet hook and into the work, and make one Slip Stitch to anchor the edge.

BEGIN SINGLE CROCHET, CHAIN ONE EDGE

Place the crochet hook into the knitted stitch, and wrap the working yarn around the crochet hook (photo **A**). This is the first step to make the single crochet.

Then pull the working yarn through the knitted stitch only. There are 2 loops on the hook (photo **B**). This is the second step to make the single crochet.

Next, wrap the yarn around the crochet hook (step 3) and pull through the 2 loops on the hook (step 4; photo **C**). In crochet, this is called a Single Crochet. One loop remains on the crochet hook.

Next, without putting the hook into the work, place the yarn around the crochet hook (photo **D**), and pull it through the loop on the hook (photo **E**). In crochet, this is called a Chain Stitch. A new loop is on the crochet hook.

Continue in this manner, alternating the Single Crochet with the Chain One across the edge as instructed in the pattern. Once the pattern is complete, cut the yarn, leaving at least a 6-in. tail, and pull the yarn through the last stitch. Weave in the end. Trim the excess.

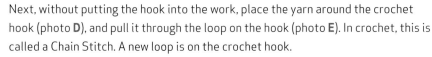

FINISHING TIPS

You'll want to finish your garment neatly so it maintains a professional look.

WEAVING IN YARN TAILS

When your project is complete, use a large crochet hook to weave your tails in and out of a cast-off or cast-on edge (photo **A**) or in areas where you've run out of yarn or changed color and added a new skein.

When there is a color change, make sure you weave the tails or ends into the matching color area so that they are less visible (photo **B**).

WHAT IS GAUGE?

Gauge is a measurement system designed to ensure that your knitting tension produces the same results in length, width, or other dimensions as those suggested in the pattern instructions. With items such as scarves and cowls, the gauge may not be as vital, but when creating a highly constructed garment where armholes or angles have to fit together, it is necessary to achieve the suggested gauge.

A standard gauge is measured on a knitted swatch using a ruler to measure 4 in. vertically (photo **A**) and 4 in. horizontally (photo **B**). These measurements determine the number of rows per inch and the number of stitches per inch. Just knit a swatch using the predominant stitch found in the project (unless otherwise indicated in the gauge specified) that is at least 5 in. wide and 5 in. long for best results. Lay a ruler horizontally on your test swatch and count the number of stitches across the row between the 0-in. and 4-in. marks on the ruler. Then place the ruler vertically on your swatch and count the number of rows in a 4-in. space. If your gauge matches the gauge specified in the pattern instructions, your finished work should result in the size described in the pattern.

LINDA'S
WORDS OF WISDOM

DYE LOTS. Yarn manufacturers assign a "dye lot" number to the batch just dyed because the formula is not 100 percent exact every time. Ideally, all of your yarn for a project should come from the same dye lot, which is listed on the yarn label. If you can't find the same yarn dye lots, don't stress; mix them strategically! For example, if you are using multiple strands, use two different dye lots to soften the sometimes-obvious color differences. Just try to buy a few of each of the dye lots so you can be consistent in your combinations. If a yarn brand does not have dye lots, the yarn wrapper will indicate "no dye lot."

WORKING IN A COLOR CHANGE. When working with different colors of yarn in a project, you can knit in the ends or tie in the ends. There are benefits to knitting in new colors versus tying in new colors. I like to knit across a few stitches with the end of one skein of yarn and the beginning of the next skein at the same time. I hold the two tails (averaging 6 in. to 8 in. long) as I work so that they become trapped within each new stitch I make. Tying a knot can be obvious, and it can work its way through to the front in projects made with bigger stitches.

CYC NUMBER AND GAUGE. CYC numbers are important, but not all yarn brands and types will knit up with the same gauge even if they have the same CYC number. If you need to change yarns in a pattern, knit a gauge swatch for each of the yarns listed.

WORKING WITH VARIEGATED YARN. When I create a project with variegated yarn, I use multiple strands of the yarn that start at different points on the color strand. Doing this simultaneously beefs up the variegation while also muting it. The result is scrumptious!

CASTING OFF IN A RIB STITCH OR ON A PURL SIDE. I try to always cast off in the stitch pattern that I am knitting unless the pattern says otherwise. For example, if I am knitting in Stockinette Stitch and the next row would be a knit row, I cast off using the knit stitch. If I am on the backside of Stockinette Stitch and am supposed to purl that row, I purl the cast-off. When casting off a ribbed edge, I do so in the established pattern. This technique creates a subtle difference in the finished edge.

PREVENTING THE WORKING YARN FROM TWISTING. When you are using multiple strands, the yarn can sometimes overtwist. There are two ways to remedy this. Option one is to prewind the yarn (if the pattern says this is OK). Prewinding will give you an even twist, and the combined yarns will act like one. If the pattern does not indicate prewinding, there is likely a reason. Option two is to "unwind" the yarn as you go by countertwisting your work—needles and all—if it gets overtwisted or to turn the work in the opposite direction every time you begin a new row.

WORKING WITH DOUBLE STRANDS OF YARN. Let's say the pattern calls for three balls of yarn that will be worked as a double strand. Simply take the third ball and measure out half the yarn, then cut it into two halves. Next, wind the two separate half sections into one double-strand ball. When each yarn ends, attach it to one of the full balls and continue winding until you have one huge double-strand ball. Note that yarn labels contain yardage information, which is extremely helpful when planning your yarn needs.

THE
PROJECTS

HIGH-LOW MULTI-STRAND SHAWL

High-low garments are all the rage on the runway, and this high-low shawl is a perfect four-season wearable because it is lighter in weight than some of the other projects in this book. I used the largest needle size available on the market, so there are large open spaces between the stitches. To stabilize the stitches when using this technique, use a synthetic yarn such as the eyelash novelty yarn I chose. Synthetic yarns are less stretchy than natural yarns, helping to keep the knitted project stable when you create a more open look. This is a great item to wear layered during the day or as a lightweight wrap on chilly nights in warmer months.

SKILL LEVEL
Beginner

YARN
Color A (faux fur): 2 skeins (a total of approximately 128 yd./117 m) polyester fur-type yarn, (CYC 5) Bulky

Color B (wool): 2 skeins (a total of approximately 212 yd./194 m) acrylic/wool-blend yarn, (CYC 6) Super Bulky

Color C (bouclé): 1 skein (a total of approximately 185 yd./169 m) acrylic bouclé-type yarn, (CYC 5) Bulky

SHOWN IN
Color A: Lion Brand® Fun Fur®; 100% polyester; 63 yd. (58 m), 1.75 oz. (50 g); color: Purpletini

Color B: Lion Brand Wool Ease® Thick & Quick®; 80% acrylic, 20% wool; 106 yd. (97 m); 6 oz. (170 g); color: Glacier

Color C: Lion Brand Homespun; 98% acrylic, 2% polyester; 185 yd. (169 m); 6 oz. (170 g); color: Mixed Berries

NEEDLES & NOTIONS
1 pair U.S. size 50 (25 mm) straight or circular knitting needles, 24 in. (60 cm) long

Yarn needle or crochet hook, U.S. size P (11.5 mm) or similar size, to weave in the ends

GAUGE

Measured flat using multistrand yarns in
Stockinette Stitch:

4 stitches = 4 in.

5 rows = 4 in.

FINISHED MEASUREMENTS

Front Piece Rectangle before connecting is
42 in. wide, measured across the cast-off edge.

Front Piece Rectangle before connecting is
14 in. long, measured down the center of
the rectangle.

Back Piece Rectangle before connecting is
14 in. wide, measured across the cast-off edge.

Back Piece Rectangle before connecting is
10 in. long.

NOTE: The back piece will be turned on its side
when connecting; this is the measurement
when turned upright.

TO SUPPORT THE WEIGHT OF A LARGER
project as it is created, I find it helpful to
use circular needles and knit back and forth
as if they were straight needles. This helps
distribute the weight of the yarn more evenly
as you knit, and it can also help to prevent
your hands from becoming tired. Both straight
needles and circular needles produce the
same finished results, so use the needles
that work best for you.

MAKE THE FRONT

Holding 3 strands of yarn together from a
prewound 3-strand ball and working them
as one, measure off 4 yd. Beginning with a
slip knot as shown on pp. 14–15, cast on
a total of 40 stitches using the Long-Tail
Cast-On method shown on p. 14, leaving an
approximately 6-in. tail after the cast-on row
is complete.

THE BIG PICTURE

As you will see in the pattern instructions,
I hold together 3 strands of yarn at the
same time (1 strand of each different yarn).
Since each yarn is a different yardage, I
suggest prewinding the yarns into one big
ball before beginning to knit. This gives
you the opportunity to attach one skein to
the next (when you run out of a skein) while
winding the ball instead of trying to do it
while you are knitting. When connecting
eyelash yarn ends, use square knots, which
are more secure.

ROW 1 (WRONG SIDE OF WORK, WS): Purl
across the row; turn your work.

ROW 2 (RIGHT SIDE OF WORK, RS): Knit across
the row; turn your work.

Repeat Rows 1 and 2 (Stockinette Stitch as
shown on p. 23) for a total of 14 rows.

**ROW 15 (WS) (NOTE THE CHANGE IN PATTERN
ON THIS ROW):** Knit across the row; turn
your work.

ROW 16 (RS): Knit across the row; turn your
work.

Rows 15 and 16 create a pattern that is
referred to as Garter Stitch, as shown
on p. 23. Knit in Garter Stitch for a total
of 6 rows, ending with Row 20. Cast
off as shown on pp. 21–22, leaving an
approximately 6-in. tail.

DESIGNER'S
BIG IDEA

I really love to combine yarns to create my own looks. It is a very creative process, and once you try it, you will most likely keep experimenting. I sometimes pick a variegated yarn first, then select coordinating solid colors found in the variegation for my other yarns. You can also try the exact yarns I used but in your own personal color palette. Yarns in a range of winter whites will make a cozy, chic shawl. I think I am going to try that combination next and will let you know how it turns out!

MAKE THE BACK

Holding 3 strands of yarn together from a prewound 3-strand ball and working them as one, measure off 2 yd. Beginning with a slip knot as shown on pp. 14–15, cast on a total of 19 stitches using the Long-Tail Cast-On method shown on p. 14, leaving a 6-in. tail after the cast-on row is complete.

ROW 1 (WS): Knit 3, Purl 13, Knit 3. Turn your work.

ROW 2 (RS): Knit across the row. Turn your work.

Repeat Rows 1 and 2 for a total of 14 rows. Cast off as shown on pp. 21–22, leaving a 1-yd. tail.

FINISHING

To connect the front and back, lay the large Front horizontally on a flat surface, WS up, with the cast-on edge at the bottom and the cast-off edge at the top (see drawing A on the facing page). Fold the upper right and upper left corners down to meet the bottom edge (see drawing B). The rectangle now looks like a trapezoid with the long side on the bottom (see drawing C). Place the small Back, RS up, in the center of the folded front between the sections that were folded down, aligning the edges. Position it so the Garter Stitch edges of the Back are at the top and bottom. Using a crochet hook or yarn needle and the Back's tails, connect the edges of the Front to the edges of the Back by weaving the tails back and forth between the two pieces as shown on p. 34 (see drawing D).

Weave in the ends as shown on p. 41.

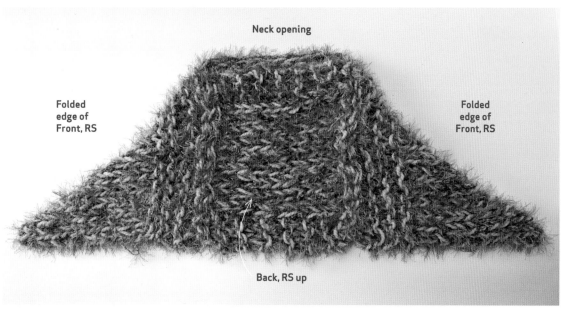

Neck opening

Folded
edge of
Front, RS

Folded
edge of
Front, RS

Back, RS up

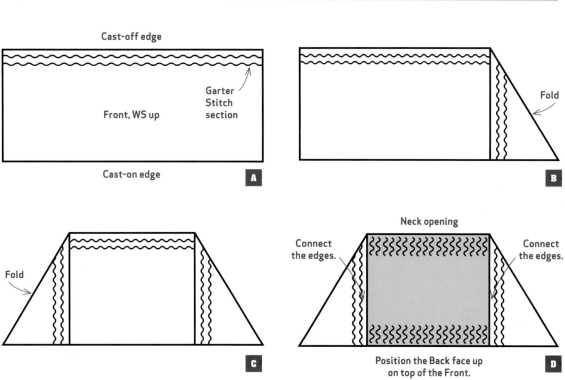

Cast-off edge

Front, WS up

Garter
Stitch
section

Cast-on edge

A

Fold

B

Fold

C

Neck opening

Connect
the edges.

Connect
the edges.

Position the Back face up
on top of the Front.

D

SHAKER STITCH
SCARF
& COWL

I was thinking about a way to create a jumbo look using yarns that may not be as bulky, and I remembered how much I used to love knitting the Shaker Stitch. This stitch creates a seriously beefed-up appearance because, in one of the pattern rows, you knit into the stitch below, which elongates the stitch's look on the surface and amplifies the rib pattern. This is a great stitch to learn if you have mastered the basic stitches and want to build your skill set.

SKILL LEVEL
Beginner to Intermediate

YARN
Color A (dark color): 2 skeins (a total of approximately 162 yd./148 m) acrylic yarn, (CYC 6) Super Bulky

Color B (light color): 2 skeins (a total of approximately 162 yd./148 m) acrylic yarn, (CYC 6) Super Bulky

SHOWN IN
Color A: Lion Brand Hometown USA®; 100% acrylic; 81 yd. (74 m); 5 oz. (142g); color: Little Rock Granite

Color B: Lion Brand Hometown USA; 100% acrylic; 81 yd. (74 m); 5 oz. (142g); color Aspen Tweed

NEEDLES & NOTIONS
1 pair U.S. size 35 (19 mm) straight knitting needles, 14 in. (35.5 cm) long

Crochet hook, size Q (16 mm) or similar size, to weave in the ends

Large clip (I prefer chip bag clips without teeth)

Sewing needle and matching thread to secure the yarn ends

GAUGE
Measured flat in Shaker Stitch with each color and number of strands called for in pattern:

5 stitches = 4 in.

4 rows = 4 in.

FINISHED MEASUREMENTS
Scarf is 56 in. long by 7 in. wide.

SHAKER STITCH
(ALSO KNOWN AS FISHERMAN'S RIB)

This scarf is knit entirely in Shaker Stitch.
I have seen various ways to achieve this stitch, but the technique I prefer is called Knit One Below (K1B). In K1B you place the working needle into the center of the stitch in the row ***just below*** the stitch you would normally knit and form a knit stitch as usual, thus effectively combining two rows of stitching into one. After you form the new stitch, remove the combined stitch from the nonworking needle. It creates an exaggerated or raised chain-looking knit stitch because it is taking up so much yarn, and it produces a thicker "fabric."

ROW 1: (WRONG SIDE OF WORK, WS): Knit across the row. Turn your work.

ROW 2: (RIGHT SIDE OF WORK, RS): *Purl 1, K1B*; repeat from * to * across the row ending with a purl stitch. Turn your work.

Repeat Rows 1 and 2 to achieve Shaker Stitch.

MAKE THE SCARF

Using 2 strands of Color A (dark color) together and working them as one, measure off 1 yd. Beginning with a slip knot as shown on pp. 14–15, cast on a total of 9 stitches using the Long-Tail Cast-On method shown on p. 14.

ROWS 1–28: Work in Shaker Stitch as described above. Cut the Color A yarns, leaving at least 6-in. tails.

ROW 29: Change to Color B and, holding 2 strands together and working them as one, leaving at least a 6-in. Color B tail, begin working in Shaker Stitch as above.

ROWS 30–56: Work in Shaker Stitch.

THE BIG PICTURE

This pattern is created using a double strand of yarn. Some knitters like to prewind the double strand into one big ball first, and in some patterns in this book I suggest that. I did not prewind in this pattern, however. Prewinding can sometimes affect the gauge, so if you choose to prewind, just make sure you are achieving the same gauge noted in the instructions. Proper gauge may not make a huge difference in a scarf, but a change in technique from the written instructions can sometimes affect the gauge and thus affect the measurements. For example, when knitting something like a sweater that fits together like a puzzle, you need to make sure you are hitting every measurement accurately.

IF YOU PUT DOWN YOUR WORK AT THE END of a row to take a break and can't remember where you were in the process, look at the last stitch on the row just completed. If it is a knit stitch, your previous row was Row 1 (above left), and you're ready to begin Row 2. If the last stitch was a purl, you're ready to begin Row 1.

Cast off as shown on pp. 21–22, taking care that you are on the wrong side of the work before beginning. This means you are casting off on a row that consists of all knit stitches across the row. Cut the yarn, leaving 12-in. tails. Using a crochet hook, weave in all tails for about 2 in. as shown on p. 41. Weave each tail separately, taking care to weave the same color end into the matching scarf section (as shown in the photo below) so that you don't see the ends on the opposite color. Trim each yarn end, leaving about ½ in. on the wrong side. To be sure the yarn tails don't work loose over time, use a sewing needle and matching thread and secure the remaining yarn tips on the scarf's wrong side.

ADD FRINGE TO THE EDGES OF THE SCARF if you like. Be sure to purchase an extra skein of each yarn color for the fringe and follow the instructions under To Make Fringe on p. 131.

MAKE THE TWISTED COWL

Follow the instructions for making the Scarf.
You will need an additional skein of each yarn color. Be sure you have at least 1-yd. tails after your cast-on is finished for connecting the cowl. You will also need to knit an additional 10 pattern rows (or a total of 38 rows) for **each color section.** Cast off, leaving at least a 1-yd. tail, and you will have a finished measurement of 76 in. long by 7 in. wide.

DESIGNER'S
BIG IDEA

Show off your team spirit with a "game day" scarf! Knit each half of the rectangle in your team's colors. Use glow-in-the-dark yarns for a game "under the lights."

YARN

Color A (dark color): 3 skeins (a total of approximately 64 yd.) acrylic yarn, (CYC 6) Super Bulky

Color B (light color): 4 skeins (a total of approximately 64 yd.) acrylic yarn, (CYC 6) Super Bulky

NEEDLES & NOTIONS

1 pair U.S. size 35 (19 mm) straight knitting needles, 14 in. (35.5 cm) long

Crochet hook, size Q (16 mm) or similar size, to weave in the ends

Large clip (I prefer chip bag clips without teeth)

Sewing needle and matching thread to secure the yarn ends

GAUGE

5 stitches = 4 in.

7 rows = 4 in.

FINISHED MEASUREMENTS

Scarf is 6 in. wide by 72 in. long.

MAKE THE GAME DAY SCARF

Divide the third skein of Color A in half and set aside. Divide the fourth skein of Color B into three sections of equal length and set aside.

Using 2 strands of Color A (dark color) together and working them as one, measure off $1\frac{1}{2}$ yd. Beginning with a slip knot (see pp. 14–15), cast on a total of 11 stitches using the Long-Tail Cast-On method shown on p. 14.

ROWS 1–38: Knit in Shaker Stitch as described on p. 54. Reminder: If you put down your work and can't remember where you are in the process, see the tip on p. 54. Cut the Color A yarns, leaving at least 6-in. tails.

ROWS 39–76: Change to Color B. Holding 3 strands together and working them as one, knit in Shaker Stitch as described on p. 54 (leave at least a 6-in. tail at the join). Cast off as shown on pp. 21–22, taking care to cast off while you are on the wrong side of the work.

Using a crochet hook, weave in all tails for about 2 in., leaving $\frac{1}{2}$ in. on the wrong side and taking care to match color sections at the color change area. Use a sewing needle and matching thread to tack the yarn ends to the scarf on the inside to prevent them from slipping out.

HOLD TOGETHER 3 STRANDS OF THE LIGHT color but only 2 strands of the dark color in order to achieve the same gauge for each color. Darker dyestuffs can bulk up yarn slightly, while lighter dyes can reduce the bulk. This is another reason why it is important to stitch a gauge swatch before you begin. Without making a gauge swatch for each color, the two ends of the finished scarf might drape or hang differently than intended.

FINISHING

To assemble, form into a Twisted Cowl as shown in the illustration at right, then weave in the tails on the short ends to permanently connect them as explained in the instructions below.

Place the knitted rectangle on a flat surface, with the light side on the left (step 1). The position of the knitted color-change join will remain in place throughout the following steps.

Wrap the light and dark ends around and crisscross the dark end over the light end, forming a circle (step 2).

Move the light end back over the dark end and "circle" it back so that the light end rests just under the knitted color-change join (step 3).

Now lift the dark end back over the light end and circle it back so it rests adjacent to the light end (step 4). Join the two ends together with a large clip and check to make sure the scarf ends aren't twisted more than they should be.

If you're satisfied, you may now join the two ends using a crochet hook and the yarn tails to create a crisscross pattern similar to lacing up shoes. Weave the tail back and forth between the ends to attach them; then weave each yarn tail separately for several inches to secure the end in place as shown on p. 41, taking care to match the color sections. Trim each yarn end, leaving about ½ in. on the wrong side. To be sure the yarn tails don't work loose over time, use a sewing needle and matching thread to secure the remaining yarn tips on the scarf's wrong side.

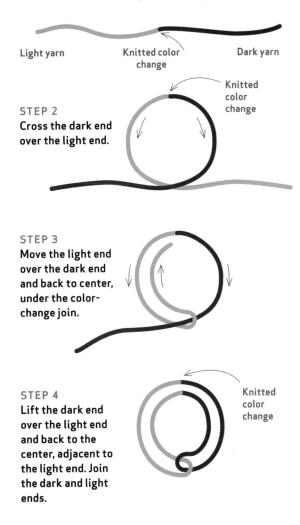

STEP 1
Lay the knitted rectangle flat, with the light yarn on the left and the dark yarn on the right.

Light yarn   Knitted color change   Dark yarn

STEP 2
Cross the dark end over the light end.

Knitted color change

STEP 3
Move the light end over the dark end and back to center, under the color-change join.

STEP 4
Lift the dark end over the light end and back to the center, adjacent to the light end. Join the dark and light ends.

Knitted color change

ROVING WOOL
NATURAL
BOLERO
VEST

This vest is the ultimate example of big knit styling. By using roving yarn, which is yarn in a very loosely spun state, the result is a highly textured look, which is very fashion forward. The varying thicknesses of this roving yarn add to the textured look, and the loft resulting from the limited amount of twist in the yarn creates super-big, visually apparent stitches. Wearables made with roving yarn look beautifully handmade, which is the goal in this pattern. This vest appears to be highly styled yet is extremely simple to make.

SKILL LEVEL
Intermediate

YARN
4 skeins (a total of approximately 88 yd./ 80 m) wool roving yarn, (CYC 6) Super Bulky

SHOWN IN
LB Collection® Wool Yarn; 100% wool; 22 yd. (20 m); 7 oz. (200 g); color: Natural

NEEDLES & NOTIONS
1 pair U.S. size 50 (25 mm) circular knitting needles, 24 in. (61 cm) long

Crochet hook, U.S. size Q (16 mm) or similar size, to weave in the ends

Sewing needle and matching thread to secure the yarn ends

GAUGE
Measured flat in Stockinette Stitch:

3 stitches = 4 in.

5 rows = 4 in.

FINISHED MEASUREMENTS
Front Pieces are 30 in. at bottom cast-on edge before assembling.

Front Pieces are 20 in. at upper cast-off edge before assembling.

Center Back length is 18 in.

Back width is 18 in. measured across the back just below the underarm cast-off stitches.

NOTE: The shape of the Front Pieces, once knitted, will look like a curved-bottom trapezoid. Later the sides of the trapezoid will be turned connected to the sides and shoulders of the Back.

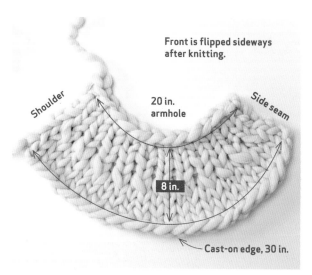

Front is flipped sideways after knitting.

Shoulder

20 in. armhole

Side seam

8 in.

Cast-on edge, 30 in.

MAKE THE FRONT (MAKE 2)

Holding 1 strand of yarn, measure off approximately 3 yd. Beginning with a slip knot as shown on pp. 14–15, cast on a total of 24 stitches using the Long-Tail Cast-On method shown on p. 14, leaving a 1-yd. tail for use later.

ROW 1 (WRONG SIDE OF WORK, WS): Purl across the row. Turn your work.

ROW 2 (RIGHT SIDE OF WORK, RS): Knit across the row. Turn your work.

ROW 3 (WS): Purl across the row.

ROW 4 (RS): Knit 1, *Slip, Knit, Pass (SKP)* as shown on p. 27. Repeat from * to * across all stitches, until 1 stitch is left. Knit the remaining stitch. You should have 13 stitches.

ROW 5 (WS): Purl across the row.

ROW 6 (RS): Knit across the row.

ROW 7 (WS): Purl across the row.

ROW 8 (RS): Cast off all stitches as shown on pp. 21–22, leaving a 1-yd. tail.

Make the second Front Piece exactly the same way.

THE BIG PICTURE

Unless you can find or make extra-long straight knitting needles, you will have to use circular knitting needles to accommodate the large number of stitches on the needle using this size yarn. You will still knit back and forth on the needles rather than knitting in the round. The circular needle length recommended is longer than any standard straight needle.

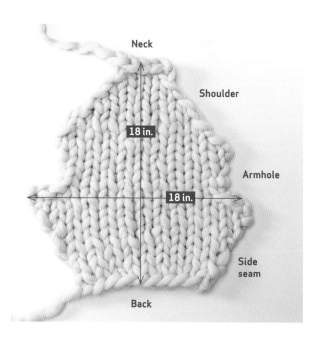

Neck

Shoulder

18 in.

Armhole

18 in.

Side seam

Back

MAKE THE BACK

Holding 1 strand of yarn, measure off 1½ yd. Beginning with a slip knot as shown on pp. 14–15, cast on a total of 10 stitches using the Long-Tail Cast-On method shown on p. 14), leaving a 1-yd. tail for use later.

ROW 1 (WRONG SIDE OF WORK, WS): Purl across the row. Turn your work.

ROW 2 (RIGHT SIDE OF WORK, RS): Knit across the row. Turn your work.

ROW 3 (WS): Purl across the row.

ROW 4 (RS): Make 1 stitch using the Loop Cast-On method shown on p. 18. Knit across the row. Make 1 stitch using the Loop Cast-On method. You should have 12 stitches.

ROW 5 (WS): Purl across the row.

ROW 6 (RS): Make 1 stitch using the Loop Cast-On method. Knit across the row. Make 1 stitch using the Loop Cast-On method. You should have 14 stitches.

ROW 7 (WS): Purl across the row.

SHAPE THE UNDERARM

ROW 8 (RS): Cast off 2 stitches as shown on pp. 21–22. Knit across the remaining stitches. You should have 12 stitches.

ROW 9 (WS): Cast off 2 stitches. Purl across the remaining stitches. You should have 10 stitches.

ROW 10 (RS): Knit across the row.

ROW 11 (WS): Purl across the row.

SHAPE THE UPPER ARMHOLE CURVE

ROW 12 (RS): Make 1 stitch using the Loop Cast-On method. Knit across the row. Make 1 stitch using the Loop Cast-On method. You should have 12 stitches.

ROW 13 (WS): Purl across the row.

SHAPE THE SHOULDERS

ROW 14 (RS): Slip, Knit, Pass (SKP), as shown on pp. 27–28. Knit all remaining stitches. You should have 11 stitches. Turn your work.

ROW 15 (WS): Slip, Purl, Pass (SPP), as shown on p. 28. (This is the purl version of SKP.) Purl all remaining stitches. You should have 10 stitches. Turn your work.

ROW 16 (RS): Decrease 1 stitch using SKP. Knit all remaining stitches. You should have 9 stitches.

DESIGNER'S BIG IDEA

A girl can always use two versions of a favorite silhouette. Have fun with your look and try this pattern with a super-big bouclé or a funky, frilly novelty yarn like the one shown here.

ROW 17 (WS): Decrease 1 stitch using SPP. Purl all remaining stitches. You should have 8 stitches.

ROW 18 (RS): Decrease 1 stitch using SKP. Knit all remaining stitches. You should have 7 stitches.

ROW 19 (WS): Decrease 1 stitch using SPP. Purl all remaining stitches. You should have 6 stitches.

ROW 20 (RS): Decrease 1 stitch using SKP. Knit all remaining stitches. You should have 5 stitches.

ROW 21 (WS): Decrease 1 stitch using SPP. Purl all remaining stitches. You should have 4 stitches.

ROW 22 (RS): Cast off 4 stitches, leaving a 1-yd. tail.

ASSEMBLY

Place the Back on a flat surface with the cast-on row at the bottom and the cast-off row at the top. Using the tails, connect the Front Pieces to the Back at the sides by weaving the tail yarn between the pieces with the crochet hook; see p. 34.

Connect the shoulders in the same manner.

Weave in the ends as shown on p. 41 for at least 4 in. and trim off the excess, taking care not to cut the work. I urge you to tack-stitch the tails with sewing thread and a needle. These are giant knit stitches, and the tails will work their way out! Just find an inconspicuous spot once you have woven in the tails, and tack the tail back to itself or another stitch, depending on where it lands.

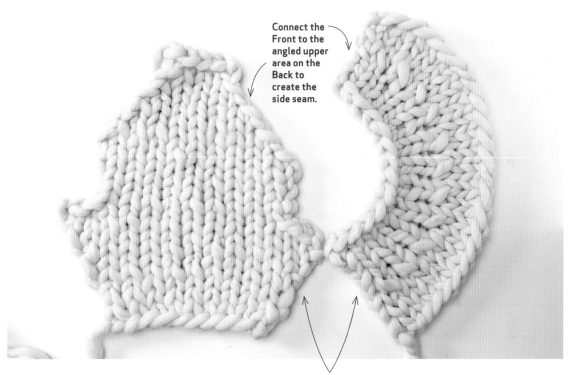

Connect the Front to the angled upper area on the Back to create the side seam.

Connect the Front to the angled lower area on the Back to create the side seam.

COLOR-BLOCKED
FAUX FUR
RIBBED
COWL

Today's fashions that feature color blocking use colors that are strong, graphic, and bold. I wanted to create a statement piece that combines color blocking and faux fur yarns, and this contemporary two-toned cowl is the result. In order to give the cowl some body, I combined the faux fur yarn with a plain super-bulky yarn to add heft and make the stitches stable. I used the same color fur as the super-bulky yarn, which amplifies the color saturation and reinforces the color block idea. There are many coordinating yarn options within each brand that can be readily purchased, so look around and choose what suits your personality.

SKILL LEVEL
Intermediate

YARN
1 skein Color A: (a minimum of 54 yd./50 m) acrylic yarn, (CYC 6) Super Bulky

1 skein Color B: (a minimum of 54 yd./50 m) acrylic yarn, (CYC 6) Super Bulky

2 skeins Color C: (a total of approximately 54 yd./50 m) faux fur-type yarn, (CYC 6) Super Bulky

2 skeins Color D: (a total of approximately 54 yd./50 m) faux fur-type yarn, (CYC 6) Super Bulky

SHOWN IN
Color A: Lion Brand Hometown USA; 100% acrylic; 81 yd. (74 m); 5 oz. (142 g); color: Detroit Blue

Color B: Lion Brand Hometown USA; 100% acrylic; 81 yd. (74 m); 5 oz. (142 g); color: Minneapolis Purple

Color C: Lion Brand Romance®; 84% nylon, 16% polyester; 27 yd. (25 m); 1.75 oz. (50 g); color: Spa Blue

Color D: Lion Brand Romance; 84% nylon, 16% polyester; 27 yd. (25 m); 1.75 oz. (50 g); color: Sachet

NEEDLES & NOTIONS

1 pair U.S. size 17 (12.75 mm) circular knitting needles, 29 in. (73.66 cm) long

Stitch markers or contrast yarn formed into a loose loop and knotted; see p. 31

Crochet hook, U.S. size Q (16 mm) or similar size, to weave in the ends

Sewing needle and matching thread for optional finishing technique

Pen and paper

GAUGE

Measured in 1 x 1 Rib Stitch with yarns A and C worked together or B and D worked together:

8 stitches = 4 in.

8 rows = 4 in.

FINISHED MEASUREMENTS

Cowl is 13 in. high, measured on a flat surface, relaxed, not stretched.

Cowl is 13 in. wide, measured at color change on a flat surface, relaxed, not stretched.

Total circumference is 26 in., measured on a flat surface around the bottom edge, relaxed, not stretched.

TO BEGIN

I found it helpful in this project to prewind the faux fur and acrylic yarns together into one double-strand ball for each color combination, especially since the yardages of the two yarn types were different. As I wound each ball, I knotted the fur yarn together to create a length that matched the acrylic yarn length. I personally find this easier to do before knitting a project rather than in the middle. Also, if you prewind the yarns to make two color balls in advance, this project is one that is relatively easy to transport so you can take your knitting on your commute, to a sporting event, or to your knitting club meeting.

THE BIG PICTURE

Knit Stitch at color change

Color change using all knit stitches across the row instead of a Rib Stitch during the color change

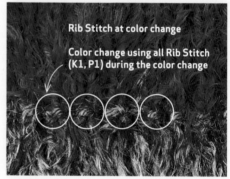

Rib Stitch at color change

Color change using all Rib Stitch (K1, P1) during the color change

Expert knitters have hints and tricks for making their work look professional. Changing the stitch with the color is a solid technique that can be done in many patterns. For example, instead of continuing in a rib pattern during the color change row, I knit every stitch. This prevents the back of the purl stitch from showing to the front and makes a sharper line, creating a graphic effect. It does not impact the stretch of the rib since it is only one row of pattern difference. Try this technique in other patterns by knitting a test swatch first.

PREWOUND BALL #1: Use 1 strand of Color A and 1 strand of Color C.

PREWOUND BALL #2: Use 1 strand of Color B and 1 strand of Color D.

BECAUSE THIS COWL IS KNITTED IN THE round, you'll need a stitch marker to indicate the end of the row. It's easy to create one using contrasting yarn (see p. 31).

MAKE THE COWL

Holding both strands from prewound ball #1 and working them as one, measure out 4½ yd. Beginning with a slip knot as shown on pp. 14–15, cast on a total of 52 stitches using the Long-Tail Cast-On method shown on p. 14. Place a stitch marker on the needle to indicate the end of the cast-on row.

You will stitch in the round. That means you'll make your first stitch into the first cast-on stitch, thus connecting your work. Make sure your stitches are not twisted around the needle as you form your work into a circle, which will connect the beginning of the first row with the end of the first row. All of the cast-on edge should be facing down, and the stitches should look consistent (see p. 31). Slide the stitch marker from the left needle to the right needle each time you reach it as you knit. It marks the beginning of each new row. Be sure to count the row just completed.

I ALWAYS HAVE A PEN AND PAPER WHEN I am knitting to make a note or two. If you get up to answer your phone or a text, for example, you should note where you are in the pattern. Believe me, this helps!

ROW 1 (RIGHT SIDE OF WORK, RS): *Knit 1, Purl 1 (K1, P1)*; repeat from * to * across. Turn your work. This is called 1 x 1 (one-by-one) Rib Stitch, as shown on p. 24. Repeat this pattern until the end of Row 14.

ROW 15: Change the color to prewound ball #2 and knit across the row. By using the knit stitch for this row, the resulting color change will appear more visibly pleasing, as shown in the photos in The Big Picture on the facing page.

WHEN KNITTING IN THE ROUND, ALL knitting is done on the Right Side of the work.

ROWS 16–28: *K1, P1*; repeat from * to *. Continue the 1 x 1 Rib Stitch pattern as before, making sure you start with a knit stitch at the beginning of each row and end with a purl stitch, moving the marker when you come to it. Here the pen and paper come in handy again to mark off the rows!

Once you have completed the instructions, you are ready to cast off. In this pattern, it is very important to cast off in the Rib Stitch pattern to maximize the stretch of the finished cowl and make it easier to put on and take off.

ROW 29: Cast off all stitches in the Rib Stitch pattern as shown on p. 24.

Using a crochet hook, weave in the yarn ends as shown on p. 41, being careful to weave into the respective matching color. You don't want the opposite color to be visible through the stitches. Because faux fur yarns can be slippery, I find it helpful to weave in the fur yarn ends as usual, and then use a needle and matching thread to tack down the yarn's last ¼ in. securely, preventing it from working loose.

JUMBO GARTER STITCH
REVERSIBLE
SWING
COAT

Of course, I had to include an oversize top pattern with a jumbo yarn! I wanted to make something super-warm that could be an alternative to a coat and make a bold fashion statement at the same time. Where I live, we are in coats so much, and it is nice to have the ability to expose our style and still stay warm. Try layering this piece over thinner knits and adding arm warmers for a truly big and bold statement.

SKILL LEVEL
Advanced

YARN
8 skeins (a total of approximately 368 yd./336 m) acrylic/wool blend yarn, (CYC 7) Jumbo

SHOWN IN
Red Heart® Grande™; 78% acrylic, 22% wool; 46 yd. (42 m); 5.29 oz. (150 g); color: Oatmeal

NEEDLES & NOTIONS
1 pair U.S. size 35 (19 mm) straight knitting needles, 14 in. (35.5 cm) long
1 pair U.S. size 36 (20 mm) circular knitting needles, 32 in. (81 cm) long
Crochet hook, U.S. size L or 11 (8 mm) for finishing
Small and large stitch holders
Stitch marker (see p. 12)

Clips (I prefer chip bag clips without teeth)
Sewing needle and matching thread to secure the yarn ends

GAUGE
Measured flat in Garter Stitch:
5½ stitches = 4 in.
9 rows = 4 in.

FINISHED MEASUREMENTS
Back is 22 in. long, measured flat from just below the collar to the hem.
Back is 28 in. wide, measured flat across the back at the widest part.
Front Side Panels are 24 in. long, measured flat from the high point of the shoulder to the bottom.
Front Side Panels are 14 in. wide, measured flat across the front at the widest part.
Center Fronts overlap 2½ in.

MAKE THE FRONT SIDE PANEL, RIGHT SIDE WEARING (RSW)

RSW (RIGHT SIDE WEARING) is a fashion industry term to indicate what side of the garment you are referring to as if it were on your body: in this case, the right side. It minimizes confusion if you learn this term and use it in your project.

REVIEW THE INSTRUCTIONS FOR MAKE ONE FRONT AND BACK (M1FB) on p. 29 because this increase stitch is used in both the Front Panel and Back pieces, and it is helpful to practice before getting into the project. You want your stitches to look even since they are super-size!

Using the size 35 straight knitting needles and 1 strand of yarn, measure off 2½ yd. Beginning with a slip knot as shown on pp. 14–15, cast on a total of 15 stitches using the Long-Tail Cast-On method shown on p. 14, leaving a 1-yd. tail for use later.

ROW 1 (WRONG SIDE OF WORK, WS): *Purl 1, Knit 1 (P1, K1)*; repeat from * to * across. Purl the remaining stitch. This is the first row of Rib Stitch, as shown on p. 24. Turn your work.

ROW 2 (RIGHT SIDE OF WORK, RS): *Knit 1, Purl 1 (K1, P1)*; repeat from * to * across. Knit the remaining stitch. This is the second row of Rib Stitch. Turn your work.

ROW 3 (WS): *P1, K1*; repeat from * to * across. Purl the remaining stitch.

ROW 4 (RS): *K1, P1*; repeat from * to * across. Knit the remaining stitch.

ROW 5 (WS): Repeat Row 3.

ROW 6 (RS): Repeat Row 4.

ROW 7 (WS): Repeat Row 3.

ROW 8 (RS): Knit across all stitches to the last

DESIGNER'S BIG IDEA

There is nothing better than a fashion item you can wear different ways. It is like having an item that clones itself in your closet—and no sci-fi is involved! This coat can be worn with the opening in the front or back, and it looks smart either way.

stitch. M1FB at the end of the row as shown on p. 29. You should have 16 stitches.

ROWS 9–13: Knit across the row.

ROW 14 (RS): Knit across all stitches to the last stitch. M1FB (at the end of the row). You should have 17 stitches.

ROWS 15–19: Knit across the row.

ROW 20 (RS): Knit across all stitches to the last stitch. M1FB (at the end of the row). You should have 18 stitches.

ROWS 21–25: Knit across the row.

ROW 26 (RS): Knit across all stitches to the last stitch. M1FB (at the end of the row). You should have 19 stitches.

ROWS 27–50: Knit across the row.

SHAPE THE SHOULDERS AND NECKLINE

ROW 51 (WS): Cast off 5 stitches at the beginning of the row as shown on pp. 21–22. Knit across the remaining stitches. You should have 14 stitches.

ROW 52 (RS): Cast off 3 stitches at the beginning of the row. Knit across the remaining stitches. You should have 11 stitches.

ROW 53 (WS): Slip, Knit, Pass (SKP) using the first 2 stitches as shown on pp. 27–28. Next, using the stitch already on the working needle left over from the SKP, cast off 4 stitches. Knit across the remaining stitches. You should have 6 stitches.

ROW 54 (RS): SKP. Next, using the stitch already on the working needle left over from the SKP, cast off 2 stitches. Knit across the remaining stitches. You should have 3 stitches.

ROW 55 (WS): Slip 1, Knit 2.

ROW 56 (RS): SKP. Next, using the stitch already on the working needle left over from the SKP, cast off 2 stitches. Cut the yarn, leaving a 1-yd. tail. Put this piece aside while you work on the other half of the front.

MAKE THE FRONT SIDE PANEL, LEFT SIDE WEARING (LSW)

LSW (LEFT SIDE WEARING) is a fashion industry term to indicate what side of the garment you are referring to as if the garment were on your body—in this case, the left side. It minimizes confusion if you learn this term and use it in your project.

Using the size 35 straight knitting needles and 1 strand of yarn, measure off 1½ yd. Beginning with a slip knot as shown on pp. 14–15, cast on a total of 15 stitches using the Long-Tail Cast-On method

shown on p. 14. Your tail will not have to be as long on this piece because it will not be used to sew up a side seam. It will be woven into the work later.

ROW 1 (WRONG SIDE OF WORK, WS): *Purl 1, Knit 1 (P1, K1)*; repeat from * to * across. Purl the remaining stitch. This is the first row of Rib Stitch, as shown on p. 24. Turn your work.

THE BIG PICTURE

Soft decreased angle using Slip Stitches at the beginning of rows

The slipped stitch used in this pattern at the beginning of an angled area of knitting, such as a gradual shoulder decrease (as shown), produces a smoother angle along the edge between row decreases. This is especially important when working with a super-chunky knit since other techniques result in and amplify a visible stair-stepped look.

ROW 2 (RIGHT SIDE OF WORK, RS): *Knit 1, Purl 1 (K1, P1)*; repeat from * to * across. Knit the remaining stitch. This is the second row of Rib Stitch. Turn your work.

ROW 3 (WS): *P1, K1*; repeat from * to * across. Purl the remaining stitch.

ROW 4 (RS): *K1, P1*; repeat from * to * across. Knit the remaining stitch.

ROW 5 (WS): Repeat Row 3.

ROW 6 (RS): Repeat Row 4.

ROW 7 (WS): Repeat Row 3.

ROW 8 (RS): M1FB (at beginning of row) as shown on p. 29. Knit across all remaining stitches. You should have 16 stitches.

ROWS 9–13: Knit across the row.

ROW 14 (RS): M1FB (at the beginning of the row). Knit across all remaining stitches. You should have 17 stitches.

ROWS 15–19: Knit across the row.

ROW 20 (RS): M1FB (at the beginning of the row). Knit across all remaining stitches. You should have 18 stitches.

ROWS 21–25: Knit across the row.

ROW 26 (RS): M1FB (at the beginning of the row). Knit across all remaining stitches. You should have 19 stitches.

ROWS 27–50: Knit across the row.

ROW 51 (WS): Cast off 3 stitches as shown on pp. 21–22. Knit across the remaining stitches. You should have 16 stitches.

ROW 52 (RS): Cast off 5 stitches. Knit across the remaining stitches. You should have 11 stitches.

ROW 53 (WS): SKP as shown on pp. 27–28. Next, using the stitch already on the working needle left over from the SKP, cast off 2 stitches. Knit across the remaining stitches. You should have 8 stitches.

ROW 54 (RS): SKP. Next, using the stitch already on the working needle left over from the SKP, cast off 4 stitches. Knit across the remaining stitches. You should have 3 stitches.

ROW 55 (WS): SKP. Next, using the stitch already on the working needle left over from the SKP, cast off 2 stitches. Cut the yarn, leaving a 1-yd. tail.

MAKE THE BACK

Using the size 35 straight knitting needles and 1 strand of yarn, measure off 2½ yd. Beginning with a slip knot as shown on pp. 14–15, cast on a total of 31 stitches using the Long-Tail Cast-On method shown on p. 14.

ROW 1 (WRONG SIDE OF WORK, WS): *Purl 1, Knit 1 (P1, K1)*; repeat from * to * across. Purl the remaining stitch. This is the first row of Rib Stitch, as shown on p. 24. Turn your work.

ROW 2 (RIGHT SIDE OF WORK, RS): *Knit 1, Purl 1 (K1, P1)*; repeat from * to * across. Knit the remaining stitch. This is the second row of Rib Stitch. Turn your work.

DESIGNER'S BIG IDEA

This swing coat would look amazing in one of the novelty jumbo yarns on the market. Try one that looks hand-painted for an artistic look. Or, if you are going for a snow bunny idea, try one of the furry bouclé or chenille yarns in the jumbo size. Just test a swatch to make sure you achieve the correct gauge.

ROW 3 (WS): *P1, K1*; repeat from * to * across. Purl the remaining stitch.

ROW 4 (RS): *K1, P1*; repeat from * to * across. Knit the remaining stitch.

ROW 5 (WS): Repeat Row 3.

ROW 6 (RS): Repeat Row 4.

ROW 7 (WS): Repeat Row 3.

ROW 8 (RS): M1FB (at the beginning of the row). Knit across 29 stitches to the last stitch, M1FB (at the end of the row). You should have 33 stitches.

ROWS 9–13: Knit across the row.

ROW 14 (RS): M1FB (at the beginning of the row). Knit across 31 stitches to the last stitch, M1FB (at the end of the row). You should have 35 stitches.

ROWS 15–19: Knit across the row.

ROW 20 (RS): M1FB (at the beginning of the row). Knit across 33 stitches to the last stitch, M1FB (at the end of the row). You should have 37 stitches.

ROWS 21–25: Knit across the row.

ROW 26 (RS): M1FB (at the beginning of the row). Knit across 35 stitches to the last stitch, M1FB (at the end of the row). You should have 39 stitches.

ROWS 27–50: Knit across the row.

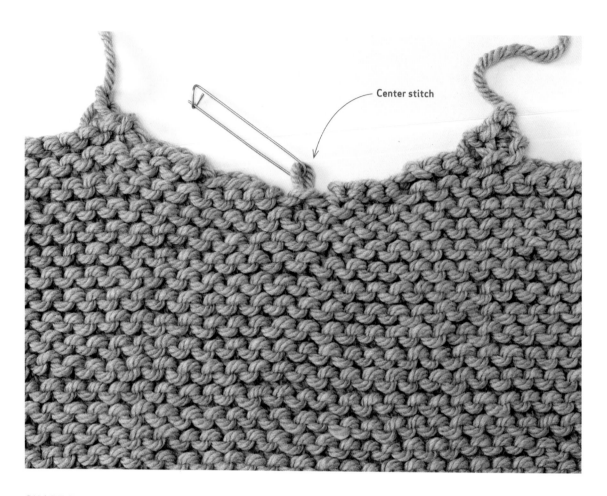

Center stitch

SHAPE THE SHOULDER AND NECKLINE

You will be working the shoulders separately, and they will be referred to as LSW Shoulder and RSW Shoulder, viewed as if on your body.

MAKE THE LSW BACK SHOULDER

ROW 51 (WS): Cast off 5 stitches as shown on pp. 21–22. Knit across 13 stitches; you should have 14 stitches on the working needle. Move the next stitch from the nonworking needle to a small stitch holder (see the photo above). This should be the center stitch of the back. Move the remaining 19 stitches from the nonworking needle onto a large stitch holder. Turn your work.

Continue working the LSW Back Shoulder as follows:

ROW 52 (RS): SKP as shown on pp. 27–28. Next, using the stitch already on the working needle left over from the SKP, cast off 2 stitches. Knit across the remaining 10 stitches. You should have 11 stitches.

ROW 53 (WS): SKP. Next, using the stitch already on the working needle left over from the SKP, cast off 4 stitches. Knit across the remaining 5 stitches. You should have 6 stitches.

ROW 54 (RS): SKP. Next, using the stitch already on the working needle left over from the SKP, cast off 2 stitches. Knit across the remaining 2 stitches. You should have 3 stitches.

ROW 55 (WS): Slip 1 stitch, Knit 2.

ROW 56 (RS): SKP. Next, using the stitch

already on the working needle left over from the SKP, cast off 2 stitches. Cut the yarn, leaving a 1-yd. tail.

MAKE THE RSW BACK SHOULDER

Keep the center stitch on the small stitch holder. Slide the 19 stitches from the large stitch holder onto the needle.

ROW 51 (WS): Cast off 3 stitches as shown on pp. 21–22. Knit across 15 stitches. You should have 16 stitches.

ROW 52 (RS): Cast off 5 stitches. Knit across the remaining 10 stitches. You should have 11 stitches.

ROW 53 (WS): SKP. Next, using the stitch already on the working needle left over from the SKP, cast off 2 stitches. Knit across the remaining 7 stitches. You should have 8 stitches.

ROW 54 (RS): SKP. Next, using the stitch already on the working needle left over from the SKP, cast off 4 stitches. Knit across the remaining 2 stitches. You should have 3 stitches.

ROW 55 (WS): SKP. Next, using the stitch already on the working needle left over from the SKP, cast off 2 stitches. Cut the yarn, leaving a 1-yd. tail.

ASSEMBLY (MUST BE DONE BEFORE THE TURTLENECK IS STARTED)

Connect the shoulder seams by placing the wrong sides together and working from the right side of the knitting. Using a large crochet hook, weave the yarn around the shoulder seams to connect the two pieces using the Overcast method shown on p. 36, taking care to create evenly spaced stitches. This adds a nice decorative stitch to the top of the shoulder.

Connect the side seams using the same method.

MAKE THE TURTLENECK

Use the size 36 circular needles for the turtleneck. Overlap the Front Side Panels at the center front neckline, overlapping the first cast-off sections of the neckline (which will be approximately 2½ in.), and clip to hold in place. I like to use chip bag clips without teeth; they are perfect for holding the work. Place a stitch marker on the circular needles. Starting at the back with the right side facing you, place the 1 stitch still left on the small stitch holder onto the working needle; using 1 strand of yarn, pick up 33 stitches as shown on p. 30, spread evenly around the entire neckline, for a total of 34 stitches. Take care to pick up stitches through both Front Side Panels at the same time when you reach the overlapped portion of the center front neckline. When you have added all of the necessary stitches, you'll begin knitting in the round. When you reach the marker, slip it from the nonworking needle to the working needle. It marks the end of each row. *K1, P1*; repeat from * to * across all stitches for 5 rows to create a 1 x 1 rib (one-by-one rib), slipping the marker at the end of each row from the nonworking needle to the working needle. Cast off in a 1 x 1 rib. Weave in all ends as shown on p. 41.

CHUNKY COWL PONCHO
WITH CABLE DETAIL

This is a gorgeous example of natural roving yarn, big needles, and a basic cable stitch exaggerated to emphasize it. The lower cable detail is worked as a long vertical shape that is then turned horizontally, and stitches are picked up and knit along one long edge to create the upper part of the poncho. It looks very complicated but is actually a fairly simple concept. Due to the natural state of this yarn, there will be variations in the texture of the final product. This only adds to the beauty of making, owning, and showcasing a handmade item! When you combine elements of various knitting techniques, it results in a very couture-looking garment. I have given this poncho an advanced rating only because of the cabling.

SKILL LEVEL
Advanced

YARN
3 skeins (a total of approximately 393 yd./ 359 m) chunky wool textured roving-type yarn, (CYC 6) Super Bulky

SHOWN IN
LB Collection Natural Wool Yarn; 100% wool; 131 yd. (120 m); 7 oz. (200 g); color: Linen

NEEDLES & NOTIONS
1 pair U.S. size 19 (15 mm) straight knitting needles, 14 in. (35.5 cm) long

1 pair U.S. size 19 (15 mm) circular needles, 29 in. (73.5 cm) long
Crochet hook, U.S. size N/P or 15 (10 mm), to make cables. A large cable needle or cable hook can be used, if preferred.
NOTE: The crochet hook can also be used to weave in the ends and connect the Lower Center Back.
Stitch marker (You will need a marker to mark the end of each row when you are knitting in the round on circular needles making the upper half of the poncho. You can purchase markers or make them; see p. 31.)

GAUGE

Measured flat in Stockinette Stitch:

6½ stitches = 4 in.

9 rows = 4 in.

FINISHED MEASUREMENTS

Center Back is 22 in. long.

Circumference at the hem is 48 in.

Circumference at the top of the cowl is 32 in.

REVIEW THE CABLE FORWARD TECHNIQUE on pp. 32–33 before beginning. Practice the Cable Row by knitting a test swatch since the yarn is chunky. Practice makes perfect and your cables look spectacular!

THE BIG PICTURE

I prefer to use a large crochet hook to work my cables rather than a cable needle or cable hook; you should use what works best for you!

CABLE PATTERN

Cable 10 Forward (C10F): Move the next 5 stitches to the crochet hook and drop the crochet hook to the front of the work (Right Side, RS), knit the next 5 stitches from the nonworking needle, then knit 5 stitches directly from the unhooked end of the crochet hook.

MAKE THE LOWER HALF OF THE PONCHO (CABLE AREA)

Using the size 19 straight knitting needles and 1 strand of yarn, measure off 3 yd. Beginning with a slip knot as shown on pp. 14–15, cast on a total of 20 stitches using the Long-Tail Cast-On method shown on p. 14, leaving a 1-yd. tail for use in finishing the garment.

ROW 1 (WRONG SIDE OF WORK, WS): Knit 5, Purl 10, Knit 5; turn your work.

ROW 2 (RIGHT SIDE OF WORK, RS): Knit across the row; turn your work. (Note: you will turn your work at the end of every row until the last row.)

ROW 3 (WS): Knit 5, Purl 10, Knit 5.

ROW 4 (RS): Knit across the row.

ROW 5 (WS): Knit 5, Purl 10, Knit 5.

Begin the Cable Pattern. Note: Row 6 is Cable #1 on the chart on the facing page.

ROW 6 (RS) (CABLE ROW): Knit 5, **Cable 10 Forward (C10F)** as described above, Knit 5.

ROW 7 (WS): Knit 5, Purl 10, Knit 5.

ROW 8 (RS): Knit across the row.

ROW 9 (WS): Knit 5, Purl 10, Knit 5.

ROW 10 (RS): Knit across the row.

ROW 11 (WS): Knit 5, Purl 10, Knit 5.

ROW 12 (RS): Knit across the row.

ROW 13 (WS): Knit 5, Purl 10, Knit 5.

ROW 14 (RS): Knit across the row.

ROW 15 (WS): Knit 5, Purl 10, Knit 5.

ROW 16 (RS): Knit across the row.

ROW 17 (WS): Knit 5, Purl 10, Knit 5.

CABLE ROWS	CABLE #1 Rows 6–17	CABLE #2 Rows 18–29	CABLE #3 Rows 30–41	CABLE #4 Rows 42–53	CABLE #5 Rows 54–65	CABLE #6 Rows 66–77	CABLE #7 Rows 78–89	CABLE #8 Rows 90–101	CABLE #9 Rows 102–113	CABLE #10 Rows 114–125
ROW 6										
ROW 7										
ROW 8										
ROW 9										
ROW 10										
ROW 11										
ROW 12										
ROW 13										
ROW 14										
ROW 15										
ROW 16										
ROW 17										

Use this chart to keep track of your stitches.

ROWS 18–125: Repeat Rows 6–17 a total of 9 more times. I find it very useful to check off each "group" of rows that is repeated to make the cable. Use the chart on p. 79 and place a check mark every time you repeat each set of Rows 6–17; when the chart is full, you are ready for Row 126.

ROW 126 (RS) (CABLE ROW): K5, Cable 10 Forward (C10F) as described on p. 78, K5.

ROWS 127–131: Repeat Rows 1–5.

ROW 132: Cast off as shown on pp. 21–22, keeping the last cast-off stitch on the needle. Do not cut the yarn; you will be continuing this yarn for knitting the upper half.

MAKE THE UPPER HALF OF THE PONCHO (SHOULDERS AND COWL AREA)

Turn the knitted rectangle horizontally and **using the same yarn** and size 19 circular needles, slip the remaining stitch from the straight needle onto the circular needle.

Pick up 67 stitches as shown on p. 30, evenly spaced across the long side of the cabled knit piece. You should have a total of 68 stitches including the original slipped stitch.

Use a stitch marker to mark the beginning of the next row (see the note on p. 77 in Needles & Notions). Connect in the round. Knit in the round for 6 rows, slipping the marker from the nonworking needle to the working needle (see p. 31) at the end of each row.

NOTE: Because you are knitting in the round and, therefore, you're always working on the right side of the work, the knitted work will result in Stockinette Stitch even though you are knitting every row.

ROW 7: Knit 8, *Knit Two Together (K2TOG) as shown on p. 25. Repeat from * 8 additional times, Knit 16, **Slip, Slip, Knit (SSK) as shown on p. 26, repeat from ** 8 additional

times, Knit 8. You should have 50 stitches on the needle.

ROW 8: Knit across all 50 stitches for 5 rows, slipping the marker at the end of each row.

ROW 13: *Knit 1, Purl 1 (K1, P1)*; repeat from * to* across all stitches. This stitch combination is referred to as a one-by-one Rib Stitch (1 x 1 Rib Stitch). When knitting in the round, you repeat this row until the pattern ends. Repeat 1 x 1 Rib Stitch in the round for 15 rows, continuing to slide the stitch marker at the end of every row. Cast off all stitches in Rib Stitch.

Connect the short ends of the cable piece together using the tail yarn and a crochet hook as shown on p. 34. Note that this seam will be worn in the center back. Weave in the ends and secure with a needle and thread as shown on p. 41.

DESIGNER'S BIG IDEA

If you have two colors of roving yarn in your stash that you like, try making the lower half out of one yarn and the upper half out of the other. The changes in the instructions would be minimal. Just cast off all of the stitches in the cable piece and begin picking up stitches with the second color for the upper half, taking care to pick up all 68 stitches. You can try a tonal look where you use two neutrals, or do one half in a bold jewel tone and one half in a neutral. I can even see a variegated roving yarn on the top half with the cable portion in a coordinating solid color that accents one of the colors in the variegated yarn.

SHEEPSKIN BOOT COVERS
WITH BURLAP BOW

This look is "knot-at-all sheepish"—pardon the pun! I love the idea of using boot covers on everyday wearables so you can change your look with your outfit. When the Arctic fashion trend started to hit the stores, I knew my sheepskin boots were just right for cute covers. If you make these covers, you'll save money, too—no need to buy that second pair of boots!

SKILL LEVEL
Beginner

YARN
2 skeins (a total of approximately 262 yd./ 240 m) wool roving or wool-blend yarn, (CYC 6) Super Bulky

SHOWN IN
LB Collection Natural Wool; 100% wool; 131 yd. (120 m); 7 oz. (200 g); color: Natural

NEEDLES & NOTIONS
1 pair U.S. size 50 (25 mm) straight knitting needles, 14 in. (35.5 cm) long

Crochet hook, U.S. size Q (16 mm) or similar size, to connect the work for finishing

1 spool (9 ft./2.7 m) 2½-in.-wide burlap ribbon, such as Offray® brand

Sewing needle and matching thread to secure the yarn ends (optional)

GAUGE
Measured flat in Stockinette Stitch before assembly:

3 stitches = 4 in.

5 rows = 4 in.

FINISHED MEASUREMENTS
Each boot cover is 16 in. wide by 8 in. high when measured on a flat surface as a rectangle prior to connecting into a cylinder shape.

MAKE THE BOOT COVERS (MAKE 2)

Holding 1 strand of yarn, measure off 2 yd. Beginning with a slip knot as shown on pp. 14–15, cast on a total of 12 stitches using the Long-Tail Cast-On method shown on p. 14, leaving at least a 1-yd. tail for use later.

ROW 1 (WRONG SIDE OF WORK, WS): Purl across the row as shown on p. 20. Turn your work.

ROW 2 (RIGHT SIDE OF WORK, RS): Knit across the row as shown on p. 19. Turn your work.

ROW 3 (WS): Purl across the row.

ROW 4 (RS): Knit across the row.

ROW 5 (WS): Purl across the row.

ROW 6 (RS): Knit across the row.

ROW 7 (WS): Purl across the row.

ROW 8 (RS): Cast off all stitches as shown on pp. 21–22, leaving a very short tail about 6 in. long.

Make the second Boot Cover exactly the same way.

FINISHING

Position the work to form a cylinder, taking care that the cast-on edge is at the bottom of the cylinder and the cast-off edge is at the top. This creates a nice top and bottom edge once finished. With the sides of the knitting touching each other, and using the crochet hook, use the longer cast-on tail to weave the yarn back and forth across the sides to connect them and form the cylinder; see p. 34.

Weave in both tails as shown on p. 41, leaving ½ in. on the inside. I suggest using a sewing needle and matching thread to sew small tack stitches along both yarn ends on the wrong side of the work to secure the ends and keep them from working their way out.

Cut the ribbon in half. Pull one length through the top of one cylinder and tie into a bow as shown on the facing page. Use the other piece of ribbon for the other boot cover and position the same way.

THE BIG PICTURE

Sometimes with these very large yarns, the knitted work falls off the end of the needle because the stitches are so big—they slide right over the knitting needle's "stop." You can prevent this from happening by cutting a piece of cardboard into two 2-in. to 3-in. donut shapes and placing one on each needle, snugging it to the end of the needle near the "stop." This should keep your work from sliding off the back end without adding too much weight on your needle.

DESIGNER'S BIG IDEA

This pattern is ideal for shorter sheepskin boots. If your boots are higher, continue knitting as instructed, going as high up as necessary. Be sure to buy extra skeins of yarn!

Instead of a burlap bow, try a textured ribbon, such as velvet or leather (available at most of the larger craft supply stores). Or use wide lace for a delicate look. You can also use your ribbon to connect the knitted piece to form the cylinder. Ribbon not your style? Rock the boot covers using only the wool. As you can see, the only rule is to have fun!

FUR AND ROVING WOOL
HAT &
FINGERLESS
MITTS

I am definitely a "hat" person! I love to match my hats to my outfits, and in the Northeast, where I live, there is the added benefit of warmth during the long winter season. I was pleasantly surprised to see high-end couture designers featuring hand-knit hats on the runway, elevating the status of handmade knitwear.

The matching mitts will take your look up a notch! It won't take more than an afternoon for you to make these showstoppers. Note that additional yarn is needed to make the mitts; look for the information on p. 88.

This pattern pays homage to one of my favorite classic couturiers. I hope you love it as much as I do!

FUR AND WOOL HAT

SKILL LEVEL
Intermediate

YARN
Yarn A: 2 skeins (a total of approximately 98 yd./90 m) 100% wool roving-type yarn, (CYC 5) Bulky
Yarn B: 1 skein (approximately 87 yd./80 m) tweed variegated wool or wool-blend yarn, (CYC 6) Super Bulky

Yarn C: 2 skeins (a total of approximately 98 yd./90 m) fur-type yarn, (CYC 5) Bulky

SHOWN IN
Yarn A: Lion Brand Martha Stewart Crafts™/MC Roving Wool; 100% wool; 49 yd. (45 m); 1.5 oz. (42 g); color: Rhubarb
Yarn B: Lion Brand Wool-Ease Thick & Quick; 80% acrylic, 20% wool; 87 yd. (80 m); 5 oz. (140 g); color: Marble

Yarn C: Loops & Threads® Fabulous Fur™; 78% polyester, 20% nylon; 49 yd. (44 m); 3 oz. (85 g); color: Lynx

NEEDLES & NOTIONS

1 pair U.S. size 17 (12.75 mm) straight knitting needles; 14 in. (35.5 cm) long

Extra-large (4½ in.) pom-pom maker, such as Clover Pom-Pom Maker, item number 3128, 4½ in. (115 mm) diameter

Crochet hook, size K or 10½ (6.5 mm), for finishing

Sewing needle and heavy-duty matching sewing thread for stabilizing the pom-pom center

GAUGES

Gauge #1: 2 x 2 Rib Stitch using 2 strands of Yarn A:

8 stitches = 4 in.

10 rows = 4 in.

Gauge #2: Stockinette Stitch using 2 strands of Yarn A:

THE BIG PICTURE

In the patterns here you will be instructed to knit back and forth on the needles and connect the sides of the knitted pieces to finish. Experienced knitters may prefer to knit these projects in the round using 4 double-pointed needles. Chunky double-pointed needles can be hard to find, but most stores carry up to a size 17. If you use them, remember that knitting Stockinette Stitch in the round does not require purling since you never knit on the wrong side, so you will have to revise the pattern.

7 stitches = 4 in.

10 rows = 4 in.

Gauge #3: Stockinette Stitch using 1 strand of Yarn B and 1 strand of Yarn C:

7 stitches = 4 in.

10 rows = 4 in.

FINISHED MEASUREMENTS

Hat Brim circumference is 20 in. around the cast-on edge after connected and measured flat.

Length is 9 in. from the cast-on edge to the top of the Hat.

MAKE THE HAT

Starting at the bottom hat edge, holding together 2 strands of Yarn A and working them as one, measure off 2½ yd. Beginning with a slip knot as shown on pp. 14–15, cast on a total of 42 stitches using the Long-Tail Cast-On method shown on p. 14. Note: You will use the remaining tail yarns to sew up the first color-block section of the hat.

ROW 1 (WRONG SIDE OF WORK, WS): *Knit 2, Purl 2 (K2, P2)*, repeat from * to * across the row, until there are 2 stitches remaining on the nonworking needle. Knit the 2 remaining stitches. Turn your work.

ROW 2 (RIGHT SIDE OF WORK, RS): *Purl 2, Knit 2 (P2, K2)*, repeat from * to * across the row, until there are 2 stitches remaining on the nonworking needle. Purl the 2 remaining stitches. Turn your work.

ROW 3: (WS): *K2, P2*, repeat from * to * across, until the last 2 stitches, Knit 2.

ROW 4 (RS): *P2, K2*, repeat from * to * across, until the last 2 stitches, Purl 2.

Continue with 2 strands of Yarn A, but switch to Stockinette Stitch as shown on p. 23 for the next 6 rows as follows:

ROW 5 (WS): Purl across the row.

ROW 6 (RS): Knit across the row.

ROW 7 (WS): Purl across the row.

ROW 8 (RS): Knit across the row.

ROW 9 (WS): Purl across the row.

ROW 10 (RS): Knit across the row.

MAKE THE UPPER PORTION OF THE HAT

Cut both Yarn A strands, leaving at least an 8-in. tail. Hold together 1 strand of Yarn B and 1 strand of Yarn C and work as one. Begin stitching with the new yarns, leaving at least 8-in. tails at the join. Use the new yarn combination as follows:

ROW 11 (WS): Purl across the row.

ROW 12 (RS): Knit 3, Slip, Slip, Knit (SSK) as shown on p. 26, Knit 6, SSK, Knit 6, SSK, Knit Two Together (K2TOG) as shown on p. 25, Knit 6, K2TOG, Knit 6, K2TOG, Knit 3. You should have 36 stitches.

ROW 13 (WS): Purl across the row.

ROW 14 (RS): Knit across the row.

ROW 15 (WS): Purl across the row.

ROW 16 (RS): Knit 2, SSK, Knit 5, SSK, Knit 5, SSK, K2TOG, Knit 5, K2TOG, Knit 5, K2TOG, Knit 2. You should have 30 stitches.

ROW 17 (WS): Purl across the row.

ROW 18 (RS): Knit across the row.

ROW 19 (WS): Purl across the row.

ROW 20 (RS): Knit 1, SSK, Knit 4, SSK, Knit 4, SSK, K2TOG, Knit 4, K2TOG, Knit 4, K2TOG, Knit 1. You should have 24 stitches.

ROW 21 (WS): Purl across the row.

ROW 22 (RS): *Knit 2, K2TOG*, repeat from * to * across the row. You should have 18 stitches. Do not remove from the needles. Cut the yarn, leaving 1-yd. tails.

Working 1 stitch at a time, pull the tails through the stitch using a crochet hook. After the tails are pulled completely through each stitch, remove it from the needle. Continue until all stitches have been removed from the needle and the yarn tails are through all of them. Pull the tails tightly to close the top of the hat. Then use the tails to sew together the upper color-block section of the hat. Use the tails from the cast-on row to sew together the bottom color-block section of the hat. Weave in all ends as shown on p. 41.

DESIGNER'S BIG IDEA

I have seen some incredible yarn combinations on the couture runways. There are also many images on the Internet to use as a source for color inspiration. On this hat, the fur element glams up the basic, traditional wool hat. Why not try reversing the sections and starting with the fur yarn and ending with the wool yarn? Or take it over the top with 3 large pom-poms on the hat? Going over the top is so trendy, and this fashion hat screams to take it all the way!

MAKE THE POM-POM

Make the pom-pom from Yarns B and C using the pom-pom maker and following the manufacturer's instructions.

FOR THIS EXTRA-LARGE POM-POM, I HELD 2 yarns together as I wrapped them 25 times around each section of the pom-pom maker.

When the pom-pom is ready to be tied in the center, use the heavy sewing thread to tightly tie it together first. The sewing thread secures the cut pom-pom strands and creates a very tightly wound, stable center. Tie off the pom-pom a second time with Yarn B, leaving the tails about 10 in. long. To attach the pom-pom to the hat, use the pom-pom tails and insert them into the center of the hat. Weave the tails in and out of the center a couple of times. Tie the tails to each other, and then weave in the ends. Trim any excess yarns after weaving in the tails.

FINGERLESS MITTS

SKILL LEVEL
Intermediate

YARN
Yarn A: 2 skeins (or 1 skein with at least 60 yd./55 m) chunky 100% wool roving-type yarn, (CYC 5) Bulky

Yarn B: 1 skein (at least 60 yd./55 m total) super-chunky, tweed variegated wool or wool-blend yarn, (CYC 6) Super Bulky

Yarn C: 2 skeins (or 1 skein with at least 60 yd./55 m) chunky, fur-type yarn, (CYC 5) Bulky

SHOWN IN
Yarn A: Lion Brand Martha Stewart Crafts Roving Wool; 100% wool; 49 yd. (45 m); 1.5 oz. (42 g); color: Rhubarb

Yarn B: Lion Brand Wool-Ease Thick & Quick; 80% acrylic, 20% wool; 87 yd. (80 m); 5 oz. (140 g); color: Marble

Yarn C: Loops & Threads Fabulous Fur; 78% polyester, 20% nylon; 49 yd. (44 m); 3 oz. (85 g); color: Lynx

NEEDLES & NOTIONS
1 pair U.S. size 17 (12.75 mm) straight knitting needles; 14 in. (35.5 cm) long

Crochet hook, such as size K or 10½ (6.5 mm), for finishing

GAUGES
Gauge #1: Stockinette Stitch using 2 strands of Yarn A:

7 stitches = 4 in.

10 rows = 4 in.

Gauge #2: Stockinette Stitch using 1 strand of Yarn B and 1 strand of Yarn C:

7 stitches = 4 in.

10 rows = 4 in.

FINISHED MEASUREMENTS
Mitts are 7 in. wide at the cast-on edge by 8 in. long before sewing and measured flat.

MAKE THE MITTS

Starting at the bottom mitt edge, hold together 2 strands of Yarn A and work them as one. Measure off 1½ yd. Beginning with a slip knot as shown on pp. 14–15, cast on a total of 15 stitches using the Long-Tail Cast-On method shown on p. 14. Note: You will use the leftover tail yarns to sew up the first color-block section of the mitt.

ROW 1 (WRONG SIDE OF WORK, WS): *Knit 1, Purl 1 (K1, P1)*; repeat from * to * across the row, until there is 1 stitch remaining on the nonworking needle. Knit the 1 remaining stitch. Turn your work.

ROW 2 (RIGHT SIDE OF WORK, RS): *Purl 1, Knit 1 (P1, K1)*; repeat from * to * across the row, until there is 1 stitch remaining on the nonworking needle. Purl the 1 remaining stitch. Turn your work.

ROW 3 (WS): *K1, P1*; repeat from * to * across, until the last stitch. Knit 1.

ROW 4 (RS): Knit across the row.

ROW 5 (WS): Purl across the row.

ROW 6 (RS): Make One Front and Back (M1FB) as shown on p. 29. Knit 13, M1FB. You should have 17 stitches.

ROW 7 (WS): Purl across the row.

ROW 8 (RS): Knit across the row.

ROW 9 (WS): Purl across the row.

ROW 10 (RS): M1FB, Knit 15, M1FB. You should have 19 stitches.

MAKE THE UPPER PORTION OF THE MITT

Cut both Yarn A strands, leaving at least 8-in. tails. Switch yarns to 1 strand of Yarn B and 1 strand of Yarn C held together and worked as one. Begin stitching with the new yarns, leaving at least 8-in. tails at the join. Use the new yarn combination as follows:

ROW 11 (WS): Purl across the row.

ROW 12 (RS): Knit across the row.

ROW 13 (WS): Purl across the row.

ROW 14 (RS): Slip, Slip Knit (SSK) as shown on p. 26, Knit 15, Knit Two Together, (K2TOG) as shown on p. 25. You should have 17 stitches.

ROW 15 (WS): Purl across the row.

ROW 16 (RS): SSK, Knit 13, K2TOG. You should have 15 stitches.

ROW 17 (WS): Purl across the row.

ROW 18 (RS): Knit across the row.

ROW 19 (WS): Purl across the row.

ROW 20 (RS): Knit across the row.

ROW 21 (WS): Cast off while **knitting**, not purling. This makes a purl bead on the front side at the top edge of the Mitt.

Using a crochet hook, weave the tails back and forth at the sides as shown on p. 34, taking care to align the rows and to use corresponding colors in each color-block section to connect the sides of the Mitts. Don't forget to leave an opening at the thumb hole, which occurs from Rows 13 to 17.

Weave in the ends as shown on p. 41. Trim the excess.

CAMOUFLAGE RIB STITCH SCARF

This scarf is a quick knit for that special someone—or yourself! Camo is a big look for women and men, making this scarf a universal favorite. I've given instructions for three versions—a short scarf, a long scarf (shown in the photo on the facing page), and an infinity scarf (see a similar result on p. 55). No matter which option you choose, you'll love the look for everyday style.

SKILL LEVEL
Beginner

YARN
2 or 4 skeins (a total of approximately 178 to 348 yd./160 m to 320 m) chunky acrylic/wool-blend variegated yarn, (CYC 6) Super Bulky, depending on which pattern you choose. There are three scarf versions, and each has a different yardage requirement. Choose the one that's appropriate.
- Short Scarf (2 skeins, a total of 178 yd./160 m)
- Long Scarf (4 skeins, a total of 348 yd./320 m)
- Infinity Scarf (4 skeins, a total of 348 yd./320 m)

NOTE: To keep the variegation consistent throughout the Long Scarf and Infinity Scarf projects, I am requiring additional yarn instead of asking you to divide a skein in half. Both of these scarves are knit with two yarns worked together as one. Hold the yarn together from 2 skeins—1 strand from each skein—and knit until you run out, then hold the yarn together from the next 2 skeins in the same manner. You will have a fair amount of leftover yarn. You may want to use it to make fringe around the bottom edges of the Long Scarf or along the outside edges of the Infinity Scarf (see p. 131 for instructions on making fringe), or hang on to it for another project.

SHOWN IN
Lion Brand Wool-Ease Thick & Quick; 80% acrylic, 20% wool; 87 yd. (80 m); 5 oz. (140 g); color: Jungle

NEEDLES & NOTIONS
1 pair U.S. size 35 (19 mm) straight knitting needles, 14 in. (35.5 cm) long

Crochet hook, U.S. size Q (16 mm) or similar size, to weave in the ends

Tape measure

Sewing needle and matching thread to secure the yarn ends

GAUGE

Measured flat using 2 strands of yarn in 1 x 1 Rib Stitch; make sure to count each stitch across since the rib pattern hides the purl stitch unless stretched:

7½ stitches = 4 in.

7½ rows = 4 in.

FINISHED MEASUREMENTS

Short Scarf is 7 in. wide by 42 in. long, measured flat.

Long Scarf is 7 in. wide by 60 in. long, measured flat.

Infinity Scarf is 8 in. wide by 58 in. long, measured flat.

MAKE THE SHORT SCARF (2 SKEINS OF YARN)

Holding 2 strands of yarn together (one from each skein) and working them as one, measure off 2 yd. Beginning with a slip knot as shown on pp. 14–15, cast on a total of 13 stitches using the Long-Tail Cast-On method shown on p. 14.

ROW 1 (WRONG SIDE OF WORK, WS): *Purl 1, Knit 1 (P1, K1)*; repeat from * to * across. Purl the last stitch. This is the first row of Rib Stitch, as shown on p. 24. Turn your work.

ROW 2 (RIGHT SIDE OF WORK, RS): *Knit 1, Purl 1 (K1, P1)*; repeat from * to * across. Knit the last stitch. This is the second row of Rib Stitch. Turn your work.

This stitch combination is called a 1 x 1 (one-by-one) Rib Stitch; see p. 24. By using an uneven number of stitches, your edges are more symmetrical because you begin and end with the same stitch on each side. If

DESIGNER'S BIG IDEA

Add some steampunk style, brass-look buttons, or decorative star pins along the scarf's edge to take its military-inspired look up a notch!

there were an even number of stitches in each row, this would not be the case.

Continue the 1 x 1 Rib Stitch for approximately 42 in., or until you have just enough yarn left to cast off and leave a 6-in. tail. Cast off as shown on pp. 21–22, making sure to cast off while still stitching in the 1 x 1 Rib Stitch pattern; see p. 24.

FINISHING

Using a crochet hook, weave in the yarn tails for about 2 in. as shown on p. 41. Trim, leaving about ½ in. on the wrong side. Using the needle and thread, secure the yarn ends to the scarf so they don't work themselves loose over time. Stitch them as inconspicuously as you can.

MAKE THE LONG SCARF
(4 SKEINS OF YARN)

Holding 2 strands of yarn together (one from each skein) and working them as one, measure off 2 yd. Beginning with a slip knot as shown on pp. 14–15, cast on a total of 13 stitches using the Long-Tail Cast-On method shown on p. 14.

ROW 1 (WRONG SIDE OF WORK, WS): *Purl 1, Knit 1 (P1, K1)*; repeat from * to * across. Purl the last stitch. This is the first row of Rib Stitch, as shown on p. 24. Turn your work.

ROW 2 (RIGHT SIDE OF WORK, RS): *Knit 1, Purl 1 (K1, P1)*; repeat from * to * across. Knit the last stitch. This is the second row of Rib Stitch. Turn your work.

This stitch combination is called a 1 x 1 (one-by-one) Rib Stitch; see p. 24. Continue the 1 x 1 Rib Stitch for approximately 60 in. or until you have just enough yarn left to cast off and leave a 6-in. tail. Cast off as shown on pp. 21–22, making sure to cast off while still stitching in the 1 x 1 Rib Stitch pattern; see p. 24.

FINISHING

Using a crochet hook, weave in the yarn tails for about 2 in. as shown on p. 41. Trim, leaving about ½ in. on the wrong side. Using the needle and thread, secure the yarn ends to the scarf so that they don't work themselves loose over time. Stitch them as inconspicuously as you can.

MAKE THE INFINITY SCARF
(4 SKEINS OF YARN)

Holding 2 strands of yarn together (one from each skein) and working them as one, measure off 2 yd. Beginning with a slip knot as shown on pp. 14–15, cast on a total of 15 stitches using the Long-Tail Cast-On method shown on p. 14.

ROW 1 (WRONG SIDE OF WORK, WS): *Purl 1, Knit 1 (P1, K1)*; repeat from * to * across. Purl the last stitch. This is the first row of Rib Stitch, as shown on p. 24. Turn your work.

ROW 2 (RIGHT SIDE OF WORK, RS): *Knit 1, Purl 1 (K1, P1)*; repeat from * to * across. Knit the last stitch. This is the second row of Rib Stitch. Turn your work.

This stitch combination is called a 1 x 1 (one-by-one) Rib Stitch; see p. 24. Continue the 1 x 1 Rib Stitch for approximately 58 in. Cast off in 1 x 1 Rib Stitch as shown on pp. 21–22, leaving at least a 1-yd. tail, making sure to cast off while still stitching in the 1 x 1 Rib Stitch pattern; see p. 24.

FINISHING

Place the rectangle on a flat surface, creating a large circle. The cast-on and cast-off edges should now be touching. Weave the tail yarns back and forth between the edges to connect them as shown on p. 34. I like to weave the tails from both ends and overlap them in the middle to secure the connection.

Using a crochet hook, weave each yarn tail separately for about 2 in. (see p. 41). Trim to about ½ in. on the wrong side. Using a needle and matching thread, secure the yarn tails to the scarf so they don't work themselves loose over time. Stitch them as inconspicuously as you can.

TO WEAR

Wrap twice around your neck for an infinity look.

FAUX FUR & WOOL-BLEND PONCHO

There are so many fun furs trending now that I just had to make my own version using yarn. I love to "paint the town red," but you can make this gorgeous poncho purely because you look good in red, you want to show your support for a good cause, or you like to stay on trend. Or, make it in black for a stunning evening look that is sure to turn heads. The results are show-stopping, and the bonus is you can say you made it!

SKILL LEVEL
Intermediate

YARN
1 skein (approximately 125 yd./114 m) variegated acrylic yarn, (CYC 6) Super Bulky

1 skein (approximately 81 yd./74 m) solid-color acrylic yarn, (CYC 6) Super Bulky

4 skeins (a total of approximately 108 yd./99 m) faux fur novelty yarn, (CYC 6) Super Bulky

SHOWN IN
Lion Brand Heartland® Thick and Quick®; 100% acrylic; 125 yd. (114 m); 5 oz. (142 g); color: Redwood

Lion Brand Hometown USA; 100% acrylic; 81 yd. (74 m); 5 oz. (142 g); color: Cincinnati Red

Lion Brand Romance; 84% nylon, 16% polyester super bulky, faux fur yarn; 27 yd. (25 m); 1.75 oz. (50g); color: Rose Petals

NEEDLES & NOTIONS
1 pair U.S. size 50 (25 mm) circular knitting needles, 24 in. (60 cm) long

Stitch marker or contrast yarn formed into a loose loop and knotted; see p. 31

Crochet hook, U.S. size Q (16 mm) or similar size, for finishing

Sewing needle and matching thread to secure the yarn ends

GAUGE
Measured flat using 4 strands of yarn in Stockinette Stitch:

5 stitches = 4 in.

6 rows = 4 in.

FINISHED MEASUREMENTS

Circumference of hem is 56 in. total, measured flat.

Circumference of neck opening is 24 in. total, measured flat.

Back is 10 in. long, measured down center back.

MAKE THE PONCHO

Pull out 1 strand of solid-color acrylic yarn, 1 strand of variegated acrylic yarn, and 2 strands of the fur-type yarn from their respective skeins. I do not suggest prewinding the multistrand ball in this project because you will "drop" and "pick up" various numbers of yarn strands during the course of knitting.

Holding all 4 strands of yarn together and working them as one, measure off 5 yd. Beginning with a slip knot as shown on pp. 14–15, cast on a total of 60 stitches using the Long-Tail Cast-On method shown on p. 14. Place the stitch marker on the needle and form the work into a circle so that the last cast-on stitch and the first cast-on stitch are separated only by the marker.

When you connect your work in the round, make sure the bottom edges of all cast-on stitches are facing down. Also make sure the stitches are not twisted around the needle. If they are, you will have to rip them out (see p. 31).

Begin stitching into the first cast-on stitch and continue around the newly formed circle. Simply move the stitch marker from the nonworking needle to the working needle each time you reach it as you knit. It marks the beginning of each new row.

ROWS 1–4 (RIGHT SIDE OF WORK, RS): Knit every stitch in each row in the round as shown on p. 31, for a total of 4 rows. Although you are working in Stockinette Stitch, you will never purl because you are

THE BIG PICTURE

Sometimes it is hard to see the stitches when working with furry yarns, and even the most experienced knitter can drop a stitch. Slowing down the knitting process so you can carefully watch your stitches will benefit you in the long run. This is a quick pattern to knit, so you will still be done in no time!

knitting in the round and always working on the right side of the piece. Since you never turn your work over, you never work on the wrong side (which is typically the purl side in Stockinette Stitch).

ROW 5 (RS): Drop the 2 strands of faux fur yarn, and cut them, leaving at least an 8-in. tail to weave in later. Some furry yarns are inherently slippery and can sometimes work their way out of the stitching, leaving a dropped stitch. I tie fur tails together using a square knot, and then tie them to another non-fur yarn in the project.

ROW 6 (RS): Continue knitting in the round for 1 row using only the 2 remaining strands.

ROW 7 (RS): Purl across the row.

ROW 8 (RS): Knit across the row.

ROWS 9–12 (RS): Continue alternating 1 row of purl stitches with 1 row of knit stitches for the next 4 rows.

ROW 13 (RS): Pick up 2 strands of faux fur yarn from their skeins and hold them together with the other 2 working yarns, leaving at least an 8-in. fur-yarn tail. Tie the fur tails onto the working yarns to prevent slippage and begin knitting by holding all 4 yarns as one. Knit 1 row around.

ROW 14 (RS): *Knit 4, Knit Two Together (K2TOG)* as shown on p. 25. Repeat from * to * around. You should have 50 stitches.

ROW 15 (RS): Knit across the row.

ROW 16 (RS): *K2TOG*, repeat from * to * across all stitches. You should have 25 stitches. The stitch marker represents where the center back of the garment will be.

Cast off all stitches as shown on pp. 21–22. Cut the strands of yarn, leaving at least an 8-in. tail of each.

FINISHING

Weave in all of the ends as shown on p. 41, and trim the excess, taking care not to cut the garment.

Because you change sections by dropping the fur yarn during the course of knitting this pattern, you should take extra care when weaving in the ends. Try to weave the fur yarn ends in the fur section and the plain yarn ends in the plain section so that the tails don't show through on the front and destroy the "banded" look. I also suggest using a sewing needle and thread to tack-stitch all of the woven yarn ends to each other since the knit stitches are so big, and the ends can work their way out over time.

DESIGNER'S BIG IDEA

If you want added drama, purchase extra skeins of each acrylic yarn and four more of the faux fur yarn (in the same yardages as called for in the main project), and knit the first two alternating sections twice for a longer poncho. Or, if you want to take the glamour meter up in a BIG way, choose a variegated jumbo yarn that has an additional sparkly thread—there are many on the market. Just be sure to check your gauge if you switch yarns or yarn sizes. Knitting a gauge swatch is a necessary step and will save time in the long run!

FULLY FASHIONED CHUNKY KNIT TOP

WITH RACER-BACK DETAIL

This top features a technique called full fashioning, which creates style lines and curves in the garment to add visual interest. It is commonly used in vintage knitting patterns to shape bodices, bustlines, shoulders, and sleeve seams. I have modernized it here by bringing the style lines up the center of the front and back, creating a very flattering look. I hope you enjoy knitting this as much as I did!

SKILL LEVEL
Advanced

YARN
5 skeins (a total of approximately 530 yd./
    485 m) chunky acrylic/wool blend yarn,
    (CYC 6) Super Bulky

NOTE: Due to yardage variations in chunky
    acrylic yarns, I suggest buying an extra skein
    to ensure you'll have enough yarn in the same
    dye lot. Most stores permit you to return an
    unused skein in a reasonable length of time,
    provided you have the receipt.

SHOWN IN
Lion Brand Wool-Ease Thick & Quick; 80%
    acrylic, 20% wool; 106 yd. (97 m); 6 oz.
    (170 g); color: Lemongrass

NEEDLES & NOTIONS
1 pair U.S. size 50 (25 mm) straight knitting
    needles, 24 in. (60 cm) long
Crochet hook, U.S. size K or 10½ (6.5 mm),
    to connect the pieces
Stitch holder (see p. 13)
Sewing needle and matching thread to secure
    the yarn ends

GAUGE
Measured flat using 2 strands of yarn in
    Stockinette Stitch:
5 stitches = 4 in.
6 rows = 4 in.

FINISHED MEASUREMENTS
Front is 18 in. wide, measured flat just above
    the ribbed hem.

Center Back Length is 27 in., measured flat at the Center Back from the top of the cast-off edge at the neck to the bottom of the cast-on edge at the hem.

Center Front Length is 22 in., measured flat at the Center Front from the top of the cast-off edge at the neck to the bottom of the cast-on edge at the hem.

MAKE THE FRONT

Holding 2 strands of yarn together (one from each skein) and working them as one, measure off 2 yd. Beginning with a slip knot as shown on pp. 14–15, cast on a total of 25 stitches using the Long-Tail Cast-On method shown on p. 14. The leftover yarn tail will be used later to sew up the sides. If it gets in the way, loosely wind it and knot it.

STARTING AT THE FRONT BOTTOM

ROW 1 (WRONG SIDE OF WORK, WS): *Purl 1, Knit 1 (P1, K1)*; repeat from * to * across. Purl the last stitch. This is the first row of Rib Stitch, as shown on p. 24. Turn your work.

ROW 2 (RIGHT SIDE OF WORK, RS): *Knit 1, Purl 1 (K1, P1)*; repeat from * to * across. Knit the last stitch. This is the second row of Rib Stitch. Turn your work.

ROW 3 (WS): *P1, K1*; repeat from * to * across. Purl the last stitch.

ROW 4 (RS): *K1, P1*; repeat from * to * across. Knit the last stitch.

TRANSITION TO STOCKINETTE STITCH, BUT START WITH A PURL STITCH ON THE WS

ROW 5 (WS): Purl across all stitches.

ROW 6 (RS): Knit across all stitches.

ROW 7 (WS): Purl across all stitches.

BEGIN FULL FASHIONING PATTERN

ROW 8 (RS): Make One Front and Back (M1FB) as shown on p. 29, Slip, Slip, Knit (SSK) as shown on p. 26, Knit 19, Knit Two Together (K2TOG) as shown on p. 25, M1FB. You should have 25 stitches.

ROW 9 (WS): Purl across the row.

ROW 10 (RS): M1FB, Knit 1, SSK, Knit 17, K2TOG, Knit 1, M1FB. You should have 25 stitches.

ROW 11 (WS): Purl across the row.

ROW 12 (RS): M1FB, Knit 2, SSK, Knit 15, K2TOG, Knit 2, M1FB. You should have 25 stitches.

ROW 13 (WS): Purl across the row.

ROW 14 (RS): M1FB, Knit 3, SSK, Knit 13, K2TOG, Knit 3, M1FB. You should have 25 stitches.

ROW 15 (WS): Purl across the row.

ROW 16 (RS): M1FB, Knit 4, SSK, Knit 11, K2TOG, Knit 4, M1FB. You should have 25 stitches.

ROW 17 (WS): Purl across the row.

ROW 18 (RS): M1FB, Knit 5, SSK, Knit 9, K2TOG, Knit 5, M1FB. You should have 25 stitches.

ROW 19 (WS): Purl across the row.

ROW 20 (RS): M1FB, Knit 6, SSK, Knit 7, K2TOG, Knit 6, M1FB. You should have 25 stitches.

ROW 21 (WS): Purl across the row.

ROW 22 (RS): M1FB, Knit 7, SSK, Knit 5, K2TOG, Knit 7, M1FB. You should have 25 stitches.

ROW 23 (WS): Cast off the first stitch in purl as shown on pp. 21–22. Purl across the remaining stitches. You should have 24 stitches.

ROW 24 (RS): Cast off the first stitch in knit as shown on pp. 21–22, Knit 7, SSK, Knit 3, K2TOG, Knit 8. You should have 21 stitches.

ROW 25 (WS): Purl across the row.

ROW 26 (RS): M1FB, Knit 7, SSK, Knit 1, K2TOG, Knit 7, M1FB. You should have 21 stitches.

ROW 27 (WS): Purl across the row.

ROW 28 (RS): Note the change in the pattern on this row: M1FB, Knit 19, M1FB. You should have 23 stitches.

ROW 29 (WS): Purl across the row.

ROW 30 (RS): M1FB, Knit 21, M1FB. You should have 25 stitches.

ROW 31 (WS): Purl across the row.

ROW 32 (RS): Knit across the row.

ROW 33 (WS): Purl across the row.

ROW 34 (RS): Cast off the first 2 stitches, and knit the next 5 stitches; you should now have 6 stitches on the working needle. Place these 6 stitches onto a stitch holder. You should have 17 stitches remaining on the nonworking needle.

ON THE SAME ROW: Cast off 9 stitches; this will be the Front Neck opening. Knit the remaining stitches. Turn your work. You should have 8 stitches.

You will now continue working to form the RSW (right side wearing) Shoulder.

BEGIN THE RIGHT SIDE WEARING (RSW) SHOULDER

RSW (RIGHT SIDE WEARING) is a fashion industry term to indicate what side of the garment you are referring to as if it were on your body: in this case, the right side. It minimizes confusion if you learn this term and use it in your project.

ROW R35 (WS): Cast off the first 2 stitches as shown on pp. 21–22 while purling; purl the remaining stitches. You should have 6 stitches.

ROW R36 (RS): Knit 4 stitches, Slip, Slip, Knit (SSK) as shown on p. 26. (Note: The SSK will make a gentle slope on the decreases of the shoulder that you will see on the next row.) You should have 5 stitches.

ROW R37 (WS): Cast off the first 2 stitches while purling. Purl the remaining stitches. You should have 3 stitches.

ROW R38 (RS): Cast off the 3 remaining stitches. Cut the yarns, leaving a 1-yd. tail.

BEGIN THE LEFT SIDE WEARING (LSW) SHOULDER

LSW (LEFT SIDE WEARING) is a fashion industry term to indicate what side of the garment you are referring to as if the garment were on your body: in this case, the left side. It minimizes confusion if you learn this term and use it in your project.

Back on Row 34, 6 stitches were placed on a stitch holder. We will now work on those stitches, and they will form the LSW Shoulder. All LSW rows will be labeled with an "L" to distinguish them from the RSW rows.

ROW L34 (RS): Transfer the 6 stitches from the stitch holder back onto the nonworking needle so that the tip of the needle is pointing toward the center of the garment. Turn your work to the wrong side once all the stitches are on the needle.

ROW L35 (WS): Using 2 strands of yarn, purl across the 6 stitches. Leave a 6-in. tail as you begin purling. Loosely weave the tail into the first stitch of the center cast-off stitches to stabilize the tail while making the piece.

ROW L36 (RS): Slip, Knit, Pass (SKP) as shown on pp. 27–28. (Note: The SKP will make a gentle slope on the shoulder.) Cast off 2 stitches as shown on pp. 21–22. The stitch remaining from the SKP will be the first cast-off stitch. Knit the remaining stitches. You should have 3 stitches.

ROW L37 (WS): Purl 3 stitches.

ROW L38 (RS): SKP, Cast off all stitches. Leave a 36-in. tail. This tail will be used to connect the Shoulder.

THE BIG PICTURE

Front

Back

In this pattern, the upper back shaping is slightly different than the shaping on the front. It has a racer-back effect and a higher neck. If you prefer, you can make the front twice for a more traditional look and a lower back neck. The chunky yarn will still add the modern fashion element.

MAKE THE BACK

Holding 2 strands of yarn together (one from each skein) and working them as one, measure off 2 yd. Beginning with a slip knot as shown on pp. 14–15, cast on a total of 25 stitches using the Long-Tail Cast-On method shown on p. 14. The leftover yarn tail will be used later to sew up the sides. If it gets in the way, loosely wind it and knot it.

STARTING AT THE BACK BOTTOM

ROW 1 (WRONG SIDE OF WORK, WS): *Purl 1, Knit 1 (P1, K1)*; repeat from * to * across. Purl the last stitch. This is the first row of Rib Stitch, as shown on p. 24. Turn your work.

ROW 2 (RIGHT SIDE OF WORK, RS): *Knit 1, Purl 1 (K1, P1)*; repeat from * to * across. Knit the last stitch. This is the second row of Rib Stitch. Turn your work.

ROW 3 (WS): *P1, K1*; repeat from * to * across. Purl the last stitch.

ROW 4 (RS): *K1, P1*; repeat from * to * across. Knit the last stitch.

ROW 5 (WS): Purl across the row.

ROW 6 (RS): Knit across the row.

ROW 7 (WS): Purl across the row.

BEGIN FULL FASHIONING PATTERN

ROW 8 (RS): M1FB, SSK, Knit 19, K2TOG, M1FB. You should have 25 stitches.

ROW 9 (WS): Purl across the row.

ROW 10 (RS): M1FB, Knit 1, SSK, Knit 17, K2TOG, Knit 1, M1FB. You should have 25 stitches.

ROW 11 (WS): Purl across the row.

ROW 12 (RS): M1FB, Knit 2, SSK, Knit 15, K2TOG, Knit 2, M1FB. You should have 25 stitches.

ROW 13 (WS): Purl across the row.

ROW 14 (RS): M1FB, Knit 3, SSK, Knit 13, K2TOG, Knit 3, M1FB. You should have 25 stitches.

ROW 15 (WS): Purl across the row.

ROW 16 (RS): M1FB, Knit 4, SSK, Knit 11, K2TOG, Knit 4, M1FB. You should have 25 stitches.

ROW 17 (WS): Purl across the row.

ROW 18 (RS): M1FB, Knit 5, SSK, Knit 9, K2TOG, Knit 5, M1FB. You should have 25 stitches.

ROW 19 (WS): Purl across the row.

ROW 20 (RS): M1FB, Knit 6, SSK, Knit 7, K2TOG, Knit 6, M1FB. You should have 25 stitches.

ROW 21 (WS): Purl across the row.

ROW 22 (RS): M1FB, Knit 7, SSK, Knit 5, K2TOG, Knit 7, M1FB. You should have 25 stitches.

ROW 23 (WS): Note the change in the pattern on this row: Cast off the first 2 stitches in purl as shown on pp. 21–22. Purl across the remaining stitches. You should have 23 stitches.

ROW 24 (RS): Cast off the first 2 stitches, Knit 6, SSK, Knit 3, K2TOG, Knit 7. You should have 19 stitches.

ROW 25 (WS): Purl across the row.

ROW 26 (RS): Knit 7, SSK, Knit 1, K2TOG, Knit 7. You should have 17 stitches.

ROW 27 (WS): Purl across the row.

ROW 28 (RS): M1FB, Knit 5, K2TOG, Knit 1, SSK, Knit 5, M1FB. You should have 17 stitches.

ROW 29 (WS): Purl across the row.

ROW 30 (RS): Knit 6, K2TOG, Knit 1, SSK, Knit 6. You should have 15 stitches.

ROW 31 (WS): Purl across the row.

ROW 32 (RS): M1FB, Knit 13, M1FB. You should have 17 stitches.

ROW 33 (WS): Purl across the row.

ROW 34 (RS): M1FB, Knit 15, M1FB. You should have 19 stitches.

ROW 35 (WS): Purl across the row.

ROW 36 (RS): M1FB, Knit 17, M1FB. You should have 21 stitches.

ROW 37 (WS): Purl across the row.

SHAPE THE SHOULDERS

ROW 38 (RS): Cast off 3 stitches while knitting, as shown on pp. 21–22. Knit across the remaining stitches. You should have 18 stitches.

ROW 39 (WS): Cast off 3 stitches while purling, as shown on pp. 21–22. Purl across the remaining stitches. You should have 15 stitches.

ROW 40 (RS): SKP, cast off 4 stitches (note the stitch remaining from the SKP is the first cast-off stitch). Knit across the remaining stitches. You should have 10 stitches.

ROW 41 (WS): Slip, Purl, Pass (SPP) as shown on p. 28, cast off 4 stitches, purl across remaining stitches. You should have 5 stitches.

Cast off the remaining 5 stitches, leaving a 36-in. tail. This tail will be used to connect the shoulders.

AS A LIFELONG KNITTER, I am constantly trying to learn how to make my garments better. One of the most important ways to do so is to learn finishing techniques. There are many ways to finish a garment, and I made several attempts on this project before finding the finishing techniques that I think make the garment look the best. The instructions follow, but you may certainly try other techniques if you have them in your repertoire. Although I encourage you to learn new techniques, sometimes the ones we are most comfortable with are the ones that get us to finish the garment instead of letting the pieces sit in a closet waiting to be sewn up!

FINISHING

MAKE THE NECK DETAIL: Using the leftover tails at the Front Neck and a crochet hook, wrap the tails around the crochet hook and pull through to the front of the work, as shown in the left photo on the facing page.

Then insert the hook into the first row of stitches to the right of the neck stitch and pull through to the back to tie in. This will add a finished look to the Front Neck edge, as shown in the photo at right above.

SEW UP THE SIDES AND SHOULDERS: Using the crochet hook and 1 strand of yarn, create a Crocheted Slip Stitch to connect the side seams in every row of the work from the hem to the underarm on both sides of the garment, taking care to align the rows on the side seams (see p. 37). Weave in the tails as shown on p. 41.

FOR THE SHOULDERS: Using the crochet hook, connect the shoulder seams by pulling a double strand of tail yarns through stitches (called mock grafting) as shown on p. 35, taking care to align the stitches across the shoulders. Weave in the tails.

I USED A NEEDLE AND THREAD at the shoulders and side seams to tack the tails back to themselves for extra stability. Chunky knits are apt to unravel because there is so much space between the stitches!

DESIGNER'S BIG IDEA

This pattern can easily be modified to create a tunic or even a maxi-length top. Just purchase 2 to 4 extra skeins of yarn, depending on the length you want, and add additional rows before you start the full fashioning. Six extra rows added just above the rib will add 4 in. of length; 12 will add 8 in. Or, try making the back longer than the front—there are some great inspirational looks on the Internet to get your creative juices flowing! I love it when simple modifications to a pattern create a whole new look. Just remember to renumber your rows so you don't get confused.

ELBOW-LENGTH
VARIEGATED
FINGERLESS
GLOVES

I designed this project after thinking about how much we use our hands. Whether we're on the computer keyboard or texting, we always seem to be wiggling those fingers! Sometimes, when touching those plastic or glass screens, we lose warmth and our fingers can become stiff. The solution: fingerless gloves! This simple pattern can be knit in a variety of yarns and is the perfect way to expand your personal style while providing the added benefit of functional fingers.

SKILL LEVEL
Beginner to Intermediate

YARN
2 skeins (a total of approximately 288 yd./ 263 m) tweed acrylic yarn, (CYC 5) Bulky

SHOWN IN
Lion Brand Tweed Stripes®; 100% acrylic; 144 yd. (132 m.); 3 oz. (85 g.); color: Woodlands

NEEDLES & NOTIONS
1 pair U.S. size 17 (12.75 mm) straight knitting needles, 14 in. (35.5 cm) long
Crochet hook, size U.S. P (11.5 mm) or similar size, to connect the work for finishing

GAUGE
Measured flat, using 2 strands of yarn in Stockinette Stitch:
8 stitches = 4 in.
12 rows = 4 in.

FINISHED MEASUREMENTS
Ribbing is 10 in. wide at the cast-on edge before assembling.
Ribbing is 8 in. wide at the cast-off edge before assembling.
Gloves are 13 in. long before assembling.

THE BIG PICTURE

When I knit a flat piece that is going to be seamed together, I always make an uneven number of stitches in my pattern. This is so that when the edges are joined, I end up connecting the same type of stitch, making the finished piece more professional looking. (Stitching two sides together absorbs 1 stitch.) Here it ensures that the 1 x 1 Rib Stitch areas remain continuous.

MAKE ONE FINGERLESS GLOVE

Holding 2 strands of yarn together and working them as one, measure off 2 yd. Beginning with a slip knot as shown on pp. 14–15, cast on a total of 21 stitches using the Long-Tail Cast-On method shown on p. 14, leaving at least a 1-yd. tail for use later.

ROW 1 (WRONG SIDE OF WORK, WS): *Purl 1, Knit 1 (P1, K1)*; repeat from * to * across. Purl the last stitch. This is the first row of Rib Stitch, as shown on p. 24. Turn your work.

ROW 2 (RIGHT SIDE OF WORK, RS): *Knit 1, Purl 1 (K1, P1)*; repeat from * to * across. Knit the last stitch. This is the second row of Rib Stitch. Turn your work.

Rows 1 and 2 make up a knitted pattern that's called a 1 x 1 (one-by-one) Rib Stitch as shown on p. 24. Continue in this rib pattern by repeating Rows 1 and 2 until the end of Row 9.

ROW 10 (RS): Knit Two Together (K2TOG) as shown on p. 25. Knit across the row. You should have 20 stitches.

ROW 11 (WS): Purl across the row.

ROW 12 (RS): Knit across the row.

ROW 13 (WS): Purl across the row.

Rows 12 and 13 make up a basic knit pattern called Stockinette Stitch as shown on p. 23. Continue to work in Stockinette Stitch by repeating Rows 12 and 13 for an additional 2 rows.

ROW 16 (RS): Slip, Slip, Knit (SSK) as shown on p. 26, Knit 16 stitches, K2TOG. You should have 18 stitches.

ROW 17 (WS): Purl across the row.

ROW 18 (RS): Knit across the row.

ROW 19 (WS): Purl across the row.

ROW 20 (RS): SSK, Knit 14, K2TOG. You should have 16 stitches.

Continue in Stockinette Stitch for 9 more rows.

ROW 30 (RS): SSK, Knit 12, K2TOG. You should have 14 stitches.

Continue in Stockinette Stitch for 7 more rows.

ROW 38 (RS): Cast off all stitches as shown on pp. 21–22, leaving a tail about 12 in. long.

Make a second fingerless glove in exactly the same way.

FINISHING

Position the work so that the long sides of the glove butt together to form a cylinder. From the right side of the work and using a longer cast-on tail, weave the yarn back and forth across the edge stitches as shown on p. 34 to form a cylinder. Continue connecting the sides up 10½ in. Weave in the tail end at that point as shown on p. 41. Now, starting at the cast-off edge and using the shorter cast-off tail, weave back and forth in the same manner as above, working down a few rows, once again connecting the sides of the cylinder. Weave in the tail. Remember to leave an opening for your thumb—as you stitch, check to determine the opening location and length that is most comfortable for your hand.

DESIGNER'S BIG IDEA

If you want an alternative and more glamorous look, try making these fingerless gloves with 1 strand of solid yarn and adding 1 strand of novelty yarn, such as the one shown, and working the 2 strands together as one. Be sure to check the CYC number on the yarn label before choosing, and always check your gauge.

This pattern can also be used to make arm covers—a fun, quick project and a fashion-forward look when you want to add some texture to your outfit but don't want the bulk of a sweater. Arm covers are also great for layering knits while wearing a poncho. You will have enough yarn from the required 2 skeins for the fingerless gloves to create arm covers instead since the glove pattern requires a little over 1 skein total.

For the arm covers, knit as instructed for the fingerless gloves, but keep knitting an extra 20 rows. Then sew the sides up all the way and let the top of the glove end at your wrist, without covering your hands. No thumb holes needed!

LEG-WARMING
LACE-UP
BOOT
TOPPERS

Put pep in your step with these adjustable boot toppers. These unique toppers have an attached leg warmer made from denim-inspired yarn and are accented with a fold-down cuff made from a coordinating bubble-type roving yarn. Whether you are wearing rubber boots and skinny jeans or leggings and riding boots, these toppers will be a perfect accent.

SKILL LEVEL
Beginner

YARN
Color A: 2 skeins (a total of approximately 118 yd./108 m) denim-like, tubular yarn, (CYC 7) Jumbo

Color B: 2 skeins (a total of approximately 82 yd./75 m) bubble-type roving yarn, (CYC 6) Super Bulky

NOTE: I only had about 2 yd. left over from the first skein of Yarn B after making both boot toppers. I suggest buying the second skein of this yarn in case the yardage is slightly off.

SHOWN IN
Color A: Red Heart Boutique Boulevard™; 73% acrylic, 16% nylon, 11% wool; 59 yd. (53 m); 4 oz. (113 g); color: Blueprint

Color B: Patons® Cobbles™; 49% wool, 49% acrylic, 2% nylon; 41 yd. (37 m); 3.5 oz. (100 g); color: Blue Shadow

NEEDLES & NOTIONS
1 pair U.S. size 19 (15 mm) straight knitting needles, 14 in. long (35.5 cm)

Crochet hook, U.S. size K or 10½ (6.5 mm), to weave in the ends

Tape (duct, masking, or Scotch® tape can be used)

Sewing needle and matching thread to secure the yarn ends

Row counter, pencil and paper, or the chart on pp. 113–114.

GAUGE
Leg Warmer: Measured flat in 1 x 1 (one-by-one) Rib Stitch as shown on p. 24, using Color A:

8 stitches = 4 in.

10 rows = 4 in.

Cuff Gauge: Measured flat in Reverse Garter Stitch (purl every row) as shown on p. 23, using Color B:

6 stitches = 4 in.

12 rows = 4 in.

FINISHED MEASUREMENTS

Leg Warmer is 20 in. long, measured flat with the cuff flipped up prior to lacing the sides together. (If you need a longer length, just keep knitting! There should be a fair amount of Color A left over after knitting 2 boot toppers.)

Leg Warmer is 8½ in. wide at the bottom cast-on edge, measured flat prior to lacing the sides together.

Leg Warmer is 14½ in. wide at the top of the cuff, measured flat before lacing the sides together.

MAKE THE BOOT TOPPERS

Using 1 strand of Color A, measure off 2 yd. Beginning with a slip knot as shown on pp. 14–15, cast on a total of 19 stitches using the Long-Tail Cast-On method shown on p. 14, leaving a 5-in. tail.

ROW 1 (WRONG SIDE OF WORK, WS): *Purl 1, Knit 1 (P1, K1)*; repeat from * to * across. Purl the last stitch. This is the first row of Rib Stitch, as shown on p. 24. Turn your work.

ROW 2 (RIGHT SIDE OF WORK, RS): *Knit 1, Purl 1 (K1, P1)*; repeat from * to * across. Knit the last stitch. This is the second row of Rib Stitch. Turn your work.

Continue in the 1 x 1 Rib Stitch by repeating Row 1 on every wrong side row and Row 2 on every right side row until you have a total of 37 rows. Use the chart on the facing page to keep track of the number of rows, or use a row counter or pencil and paper.

Cut Color A, leaving at least a 12-in. tail.

Continue the topper using 1 strand of Color B. Leave at least a 12-in. tail when you begin the row.

ROW 38 (RS): Using 1 strand of Color B, *K1, P1*; repeat from * to * across. Knit the last stitch.

ROW 39 (WS): Purl across the row. Note: This row specifically allows the cuff to fold down.

You will purl the next 11 rows, which will create a Reverse Garter Stitch pattern. Use the chart on p. 114 to keep track of the rows. Check off each row when complete. There are two columns, one for each boot topper.

ROW 51 (WS): Cast off all stitches as shown on pp. 21–22, using knit stitch as you cast off. Cut the yarn, leaving a 5-in. tail. Weave in the tail and secure the end as shown on p. 41.

Make a second Boot Topper exactly the same way.

ROW#	SIDE	STITCH	BOOT TOPPER A	BOOT TOPPER B
ROW 3	WS	As Row 1		
ROW 4	RS	As Row 2		
ROW 5	WS	As Row 1		
ROW 6	RS	As Row 2		
ROW 7	WS	As Row 1		
ROW 8	RS	As Row 2		
ROW 9	WS	As Row 1		
ROW 10	RS	As Row 2		
ROW 11	WS	As Row 1		
ROW 12	RS	As Row 2		
ROW 13	WS	As Row 1		
ROW 14	RS	As Row 2		
ROW 15	WS	As Row 1		
ROW 16	RS	As Row 2		
ROW 17	WS	As Row 1		
ROW 18	RS	As Row 2		
ROW 19	WS	As Row 1		
ROW 20	RS	As Row 2		

ROW#	SIDE	STITCH	BOOT TOPPER A	BOOT TOPPER B
ROW 21	WS	As Row 1		
ROW 22	RS	As Row 2		
ROW 23	WS	As Row 1		
ROW 24	RS	As Row 2		
ROW 25	WS	As Row 1		
ROW 26	RS	As Row 2		
ROW 27	WS	As Row 1		
ROW 28	RS	As Row 2		
ROW 29	WS	As Row 1		
ROW 30	RS	As Row 2		
ROW 31	WS	As Row 1		
ROW 32	RS	As Row 2		
ROW 33	WS	As Row 1		
ROW 34	RS	As Row 2		
ROW 35	WS	As Row 1		
ROW 36	RS	As Row 2		
ROW 37	WS	As Row 1		

THE BIG PICTURE

Not all legs are shaped the same, so here's a tip about how to make these fit you. (You may want to buy 1 more skein of each yarn if you think any width or length changes may be necessary.) Measure both the widest and narrowest parts of your leg to "split the difference" when making your changes. You want the leg warmer portion to be snug enough to fit inside your boot, yet not be too stretched across the wider area and distort the rib.

Looking at the gauge, you can see that adding an extra 9 stitches would "grow" the width of the leg warmer by 4 in. So if you add 4 stitches, the width of the Rib Stitch portion will grow a little less than 2 in. In terms of the height of the garment, 5 additional rows would elongate the Rib Stitch portion by 2 in. more. So if your legs are longer, use the finished measurements provided above to determine if you need to add additional rows to the garment. It's best to add rows in multiples of two so that the RS/WS sequencing isn't altered.

The laces make the boot toppers perfect for adjusting to various leg shapes as well. Just leave the laces a little looser at the top or wherever you need extra room. Since it is very trendy to layer knits over knits or knits over lace, allowing something to peek through the laces just adds to your fashion statement!

ROW#	BOOT TOPPER A	BOOT TOPPER B
ROW 40 (RS): Purl across all stitches. Turn your work.		
ROW 41 (WS): Purl across all stitches. Turn your work.		
ROW 42 (RS): Purl across all stitches. Turn your work.		
ROW 43 (WS): Purl across all stitches. Turn your work.		
ROW 44 (RS): Purl across all stitches. Turn your work.		
ROW 45 (WS): Purl across all stitches. Turn your work.		
ROW 46 (RS): Purl across all stitches. Turn your work.		
ROW 47 (WS): Purl across all stitches. Turn your work.		
ROW 48 (RS): Purl across all stitches. Turn your work.		
ROW 49 (WS): Purl across all stitches. Turn your work.		
ROW 50 (RS): Purl across all stitches. Turn your work.		

FINISHING

Weave in and secure all cast-on and cast-off tails and Color A and Color B tails at the yarn changes as shown on p. 35.

MAKE THE LACES

When weaving chunky yarns in and out of a side seam or creating the laced detail, I always put a little tape around the yarn's tip to keep the yard end stiff, so it can act like a needle. I like duct tape, but just about any tape will work. You'll find it much easier to weave the yarn in and out of the rows using this simple technique, and you can just cut it off when you are finished.

Measure and cut two 2½-yd. lengths of Color B. These will be used as the laces. Wrap a piece of tape around each end to help ease the lacing process (see the photo above left).

Place one Boot Topper on a flat surface vertically with the right side facing down. Form the topper into a tube, taking care to make sure that the right side is facing out. Using one of the laces, connect the long sides, weaving the yarn back and forth between rows as follows:

Place the lace tips into the first stitch of the first row—one lace tip on each long edge. Push each lace from back to front through the third row on the same side and pull it back out (A in the photo above right). Make sure the laces stay the same length on each side as you progress (B in the photo above right). Next, crisscross the laces and count up 5 rows. Place the laces down into that row and back out 2 rows above.

Continue in this manner until both long sides are connected, including the cuff area. Tie

the remaining lacing ends into a bow. Cut off the tape and tie small knots at the end of each lace.

DESIGNER'S
BIG IDEA

If you prefer a sleeker look, you can make the entire project out of the denim-inspired flat yarn (Color A) without using Color B at all for the laces. Just make this minor adjustment: Keep knitting in Rib Stitch for 50 rows (or more). Then cast off leaving longer tails, sew the sides closed by weaving the tail yarns in and out, and then fold the top portion of the boot topper down twice to create a thick cuff. You will have to purchase an additional skein of Color A, but you will not need Color B for the all-rib version. Or, instead of sewing the sides closed, add buttons and yarn loops or equestrian-inspired fasteners along one side of the final 10 or so rows of the long edges, if your budget allows, for a true designer look.

SEQUINED THROW-OVER WRAP

The pattern for this wrap is one you'll use over and over again. I designed it with an SSK (Slip, Slip, Knit) and a K2TOG (Knit Two Together) on either side of a center stitch to create a deep V, so you can wear the garment a couple of different ways. The novelty yarn I chose has sequins, giving this cape a glam effect, but you can select something different to suit a more casual style. No matter what yarn you choose, I recommend using circular needles when knitting to distribute the weight of the yarn.

SKILL LEVEL
Advanced

YARN
3 skeins (a total of approximately 261 yd./ 240 m) acrylic/wool blend variegated-type yarn, (CYC 6) Super Bulky

1 to 2 skeins (a total of approximately 202 yd./185 m to 404 yd./370 m) novelty sequin-type yarn, (CYC 4) Medium

NOTE: 1 skein of this yardage is sufficient if you're knitting a garment without the decorative crocheted edging.

SHOWN IN
Lion Brand Wool-Ease Thick & Quick; 80% acrylic, 20% wool; 87 yd. (80 m); 5 oz. (140 g); color: Marble

Red Heart Boutique Swanky™; 62% acrylic, 38% polyester; 202 yd. (185 m); 3.5 oz. (100 g); color: Sterling

NEEDLES & NOTIONS
1 pair U.S. size 19 (15 mm) circular knitting needles, 29 in. (74 cm) long (required for number of stitches, but you'll knit back and forth as if using straight needles rather than in the round)

Crochet hook, size H or 8 (5 mm) or similar size, for crocheting the edging detail (optional)

GAUGE
Measured flat and stitched with 1 strand of each yarn held together in Stockinette Stitch:

7 stitches = 4 in.

9 rows = 4 in.

FINISHED MEASUREMENTS

The finished shape is a modified trapezoid.

Wrap is 16 in. long measured flat and vertically from the top edge to the bottom along the side (straight edge).

Wrap is 22 in. wide on the half (44 in. total) measured flat along the cast-off edge (neckline).

Wrap is 34 in. wide on the half (68 in. total) measured flat along the cast-on edge of the trapezoid (hemline).

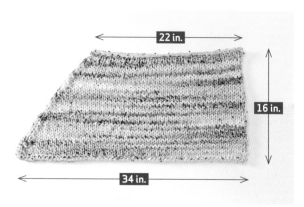

MAKE THE WRAP

Holding 1 strand of variegated yarn and 1 strand of novelty yarn together and working them as one, measure off 2 yd. Beginning with a slip knot as shown on pp. 14–15, cast on a total of 117 stitches using the Long-Tail Cast-On method shown on p. 14. Leave at least a 6-in. tail for use later. Turn your work; you will be knitting back and forth on circular needles to help manage the weight of the project.

ROW 1 (WRONG SIDE OF WORK, WS): Purl 117; turn your work.

ROW 2 (RIGHT SIDE OF WORK, RS): Knit 56, Slip, Slip, Knit (SSK) as shown on p. 26, Knit 1, Knit Two Together (K2TOG) as shown on p. 25, Knit 56. You should have 115 stitches; turn your work.

ROW 3 (WS): Purl across the row.

ROW 4 (RS): Knit 55, SSK, Knit 1, K2TOG, Knit 55. You should have 113 stitches.

ROW 5 (WS): Purl across the row.

ROW 6 (RS): Knit 54, SSK, Knit 1, K2TOG, Knit 54. You should have 111 stitches.

ROW 7 (WS): Purl across the row.

ROW 8 (RS): Knit 53, SSK, Knit 1, K2TOG, Knit 53. You should have 109 stitches.

ROW 9 (WS): Purl across the row.

ROW 10 (RS): Knit 52, SSK, Knit 1, K2TOG, Knit 52. You should have 107 stitches.

ROW 11 (WS): Purl across the row.

ROW 12 (RS): Knit 51, SSK, Knit 1, K2TOG, Knit 51. You should have 105 stitches.

ROW 13 (WS): Purl across the row.

ROW 14 (RS): Knit 50, SSK, Knit 1, K2TOG, Knit 50. You should have 103 stitches.

ROW 15 (WS): Purl across the row.

ROW 16 (RS): Knit 49, SSK, Knit 1, K2TOG, Knit 49. You should have 101 stitches.

ROW 17 (WS): Purl across the row.

ROW 18 (RS): Knit 48, SSK, Knit 1, K2TOG, Knit 48. You should have 99 stitches.

ROW 19 (WS): Purl across the row.

ROW 20 (RS): Knit 47, SSK, Knit 1, K2TOG, Knit 47. You should have 97 stitches.

ROW 21 (WS): Purl across the row.

ROW 22 (RS): Knit 46, SSK, Knit 1, K2TOG, Knit 46. You should have 95 stitches.

ROW 23 (WS): Purl across the row.

ROW 24 (RS): Knit 45, SSK, Knit 1, K2TOG, Knit 45. You should have 93 stitches.

ROW 25 (WS): Purl across the row.

ROW 26 (RS): Knit 44, SSK, Knit 1, K2TOG, Knit 44. You should have 91 stitches.

ROW 27 (WS): Purl across the row.

ROW 28 (RS): Knit 43, SSK, Knit 1, K2TOG, Knit 43. You should have 89 stitches.

ROW 29 (WS): Purl across the row.

ROW 30 (RS): Knit 42, SSK, Knit 1, K2TOG, Knit 42. You should have 87 stitches.

ROW 31 (WS): Purl across the row.

NOTE PATTERN CHANGE

ROW 32 (RS): With 87 stitches on the needle, complete the following stitch combinations:

Knit 8, then knit Pattern A: *(SSK, Knit 1, K2TOG, Knit 2)*, repeat from * to * 3 more times (a total of 4 times).

Then knit Pattern B: **(SSK, Knit 1, K2TOG)**, repeat from ** to ** 2 more times.

Then knit Pattern C: ***(K2, SSK, Knit 1, K2TOG)***, repeat from *** to *** 3 more times.

Knit 8. You should have 65 stitches.

ROW 33 (WS): Purl across the row.

ROW 34 (RS): Cast off as shown on pp. 21–22. Cut the yarn, leaving at least a 6-in. tail. Weave in the tails, as shown on p. 41.

ADD THE CROCHET EDGING (OPTIONAL)

In order to add the crochet edging, you will need to know how to complete the Chain Stitch, Slip Stitch, and Single Crochet Stitch. Detailed instructions on how to create these stitches can be found on pp. 37–41.

Divide the second skein of novelty yarn into three even amounts. Holding 3 strands of yarn together and working them as one, complete the following crochet pattern around all edges.

Beginning on one long side, Single Crochet, Chain One into each knitted stitch along the edge. When you reach the end of the side, Single Crochet, Chain One 3 times into the same corner stitch to create a rounded corner in the border (see the photo below left).

Repeat until the border has been added to the entire perimeter. When you finish all sides and reach your first Single Crochet, Slip Stitch into the top of the first Single Crochet to complete the border. Cut the yarn, leaving at least a 6-in. tail. Weave in the tails.

THE BIG PICTURE

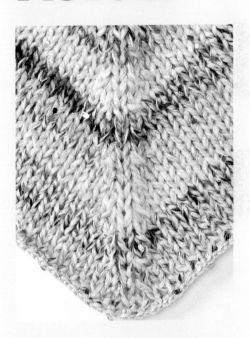

By starting out with an uneven number of stitches when you cast on and decreasing on either side of the center stitch as you knit the rows, you create a V effect as pictured. It is dramatic in this garment because you follow this technique for so many rows. Try turning the wrap and wearing the V down your center back.

GARTER STITCH
CHENILLE
TWIST-BACK
TOP

I sometimes like to shape bulky knits to the body, constructing open areas as a way to contrast the increase in visual weight. The result looks couture. This garment has the added twist of an open back, which also decreases bulk visually. This top would look beautiful and very Victoriana with a beautiful lace garment under it, peeking through the back.

SKILL LEVEL
Advanced

YARN
7 skeins (a total of approximately 385 yd./ 352 m) chenille-type nylon yarn, (CYC 6) Super Bulky

SHOWN IN
Lion Brand Quick & Cozy; 100% nylon; 55 yd. (50 m); 3.5 oz. (100 g); color: Lemon

NEEDLES & NOTIONS
1 pair U.S. Size 35 (19 mm) straight knitting needles, 14 in. (35.5 cm) long
Crochet hook, U.S. size Q (16 mm) or similar size, to weave in the ends and connect the pieces
Clips to hold the pieces together while assembling (I prefer chip bag clips without teeth)

Sewing needle and matching thread to tack the ends in place

GAUGE
Measured flat using 2 strands of yarn in Garter Stitch:
4½ stitches = 4 in.
6 rows = 4 in.

FINISHED MEASUREMENTS
Front Panels are 12 in. wide, measured flat at the cast-on edge and 24 in. long from the high point of the shoulder to the hem.
Lower Back is 13 in. long, measured flat from the cast-on to the cast-off edges, down the center of the lower back.
Upper Back is 10 in. wide by 22 in. long, measured flat from the cast-on to the cast-off edge, in rectangle form, before "twisting."

MAKE THE UPPER BACK

Holding 2 strands of yarn together (one from each skein) and working them as one, measure off 2 yd. Beginning with a slip knot as shown on pp. 14–15, cast on a total of 11 stitches using the Long-Tail Cast-On method shown on p. 14.

ROWS 1–32: Knit across each row in Garter Stitch as shown on p. 23. Cast off all stitches as shown on pp. 21–22. Cut the yarns, leaving 1-yd. tails. Set aside. The knitted rectangle will be twisted when it is attached to the other pieces (see detail A in the bottom left photo).

MAKE THE LOWER BACK

Holding 2 strands of yarn together (one from each skein) and working them as one, measure off 2 yd. Beginning with a slip knot as shown on pp. 14–15, cast on a total of 20 stitches using the Long-Tail Cast-On method shown on p. 14.

ROWS 1 AND 2: Knit across each row to begin Garter Stitch. Turn your work.

ROW 3 (WRONG SIDE OF WORK, WS): Slip, Slip, Knit (SSK) as shown on p. 26, Knit 16, Knit Two Together (K2TOG) as shown on p. 25. You should have 18 stitches.

ROWS 4–8: Knit across each row in Garter Stitch.

ROW 9 (WS): SSK, Knit 14, K2TOG. You should have 16 stitches.

ROWS 10–14: Knit across each row in Garter Stitch.

ROW 15 (WS): SSK, Knit 12, K2TOG. You should have 14 stitches.

ROWS 16–18: Knit across each row in Garter Stitch.

ROW 19 (WS): Cast off all stitches. Cut the yarns, leaving 1-yd. tails. Set your work aside. It will look like a trapezoid and therefore be slightly angled on the sides, as shown in detail B in the bottom left photo.

Long edge of Upper Back Panel

Upper Back Panel

A

B

Right Side Wearing (RSW) Front Panel

DESIGNER'S BIG IDEA

It is very helpful to review all of the shapes and illustrations before beginning to knit a garment such as this one. The instructions will make more sense, and the final result will not be as intimidating. This pattern is made from four shapes—a rectangle that is flipped at one corner to create the Upper Back, a trapezoid shape that is the Lower Back, and two Front Panels that are mirror images of each other, referred to as the left side wearing (LSW) and right side wearing (RSW) front panels. Also, when assembling the garment, I used 2 strands of yarn to connect. I found it added stability at the seam.

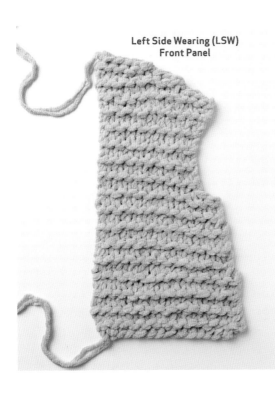

Left Side Wearing (LSW)
Front Panel

MAKE THE RIGHT SIDE WEARING (RSW) FRONT PANEL

RSW (RIGHT SIDE WEARING) is a fashion industry term to indicate what side of the garment you are referring to as if it were on your body: in this case, the right side. It minimizes confusion if you learn this term and use it in your project.

Holding 2 strands of yarn together (one from each skein) and working them as one, measure off 2 yd. Beginning with a slip knot as shown on pp. 14–15, cast on a total of 15 stitches using the Long-Tail Cast-On method shown on p. 14.

ROW 1 (WRONG SIDE OF WORK, WS): Knit across the row to begin Garter Stitch as shown on p. 23. Turn your work.

ROW 2 (RIGHT SIDE OF WORK, RS): Knit across the row. Turn your work.

ROW 3 (WS): Slip, Slip, Knit (SSK) as shown on p. 26, Knit 13. You should have 14 stitches.

ROWS 4-8: Knit across each row in Garter Stitch.

ROW 9 (WS): SSK, Knit 12. You should have 13 stitches.

ROWS 10-14: Knit across each row in Garter Stitch.

ROW 15 (WS): SSK, Knit 11. You should have 12 stitches.

ROWS 16-18: Knit each row in Garter Stitch.

SHAPE THE RSW UNDERARM

ROW 19 (WS): Cast off 2 stitches as shown on pp. 21–22, knit across the remaining 9 stitches. You should have 10 stitches.

ROWS 20-24: Knit across each row in Garter Stitch. You should have 10 stitches.

SHAPE THE RSW SHOULDER

ROW 25 (WS): Make One Front and Back (M1FB) as shown on p. 29. Knit 9. You should have 11 stitches.

ROW 26 (RS): Knit across the row.

ROW 27 (WS): M1FB, Knit 10. You should have 12 stitches.

ROW 28 (RS): Knit across the row.

ROW 29 (WS): Knit across the row.

ROW 30 (RS): Knit across the row.

ROW 31 (WS): Cast off 3 stitches, knit across the remaining stitches. You should have 9 stitches.

ROW 32 (RS): Knit across the row.

ROW 33 (WS): Slip, Knit, Pass (SKP) as shown on pp. 27–28, cast off 2 stitches. The stitch remaining from the SKP is the first knit stitch when you cast off. Knit across the remaining stitches. You should have 6 stitches.

ROW 34 (RS): Knit across the row.

ROW 35 (WS): SKP, cast off the remaining stitches. The stitch remaining from the SKP is the first knit stitch when you cast off. Cut the yarns, leaving 1-yd. tails.

MAKE THE LEFT SIDE WEARING (LSW) FRONT PANEL

LSW (LEFT SIDE WEARING) is a fashion industry term to indicate what side of the garment you are referring to as if the garment were on your body: in this case, the left side. It minimizes confusion if you learn this term and use it in your project.

Holding 2 strands of yarn together (one from each skein) and working them as one, measure off 2 yd. Beginning with a slip knot as shown on pp. 14–15, cast on a total of 15 stitches using the Long-Tail Cast-On method shown on p. 14.

ROW 1 (WS): Knit across the row to begin Garter Stitch. Turn your work.

ROW 2 (RS): Knit across the row. Turn your work.

ROW 3 (WS): Knit 13, Knit Two Together (K2TOG) as shown on p. 25. You should have 14 stitches.

ROWS 4–8: Knit across each row in Garter Stitch.

ROW 9 (WS): Knit 12, K2TOG. You should have 13 stitches.

ROWS 10–14: Knit across each row in Garter Stitch.

ROW 15 (WS): Knit 11, K2TOG. You should have 12 stitches.

ROWS 16–17: Knit across each row in Garter Stitch.

SHAPE THE LSW UNDERARM

ROW 18 (RS): Cast off the first 2 stitches, knit across the remaining stitches. You should have 10 stitches.

ROWS 19–25: Knit across the row.

SHAPE THE LSW SHOULDER

ROW 26 (RS): Make One Front and Back (M1FB) as shown on p. 29, Knit 9. You should have 11 stitches.

ROW 27 (WS): Knit across the row.

ROW 28 (RS): M1FB, Knit 10. You should have 12 stitches.

ROW 29 (WS): Knit across the row.

ROW 30 (RS): Cast off 3 stitches, knit across the remaining stitches. You should have 9 stitches.

ROW 31 (WS): Knit across the row.

ROW 32 (RS): Slip, Knit, Pass (SKP) as shown on pp. 27–28, cast off 2 stitches. The stitch remaining after the SKP is one of the knit stitches in your first cast-off. Knit across the remaining 5 stitches. You should have 6 stitches.

ROW 33 (WS): Knit across the row.

ROW 34 (RS): SKP, cast off the remaining stitches. The stitch remaining after the SKP is one of the knit stitches in your first cast-off. Cut the yarns, leaving 1-yd. tails.

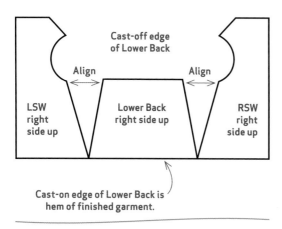

Cast-off edge
of Lower Back

Align   Align

LSW
right
side up

Lower Back
right side up

RSW
right
side up

Cast-on edge of Lower Back is
hem of finished garment.

Connect point A to point B by flipping the corner down, creating a twist.

Connect the shoulder to the Upper Back.

Align area 1 to area 2 to connect and create the shoulder seam.

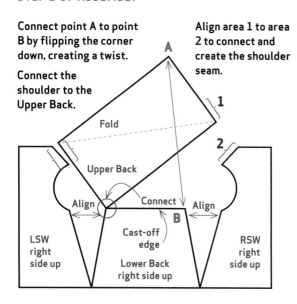

A

Fold

1

2

Upper Back

Align   Connect   Align

B

Cast-off
edge

LSW
right
side up

Lower Back
right side up

RSW
right
side up

CONNECT THE FRONT PIECES TO THE LOWER BACK (STEP 1)

Using the crochet hook and tail yarns, connect the Lower Back to the lower areas of the Front Panels, creating the side seams. Match hems and align the underarm shaping to the top corners of the upper edge of the trapezoid shape. Weave in the ends as shown on p. 41.

CONNECT THE SHOULDERS TO THE UPPER BACK (STEP 2)

Position the Upper Back rectangle on a flat surface in between the two Front Panels and above the Lower Back, as indicated in the lower drawing at left. Twist the Upper Back rectangle one-half turn in the middle as shown in the diagram, indicated with the red arrow, bringing point A to point B as shown. Hold the twist in place with a clip. Align the upper long edge (indicated by the numeral 1 in the diagram) of the Upper Back to the RSW Front Panel shoulder (indicated by numeral 2 in the diagram) as shown. Clip in place. Align the upper long edge (left side) of the Upper Back panel to the LSW Front Panel shoulder (maintaining the twist in the center) as shown. Clip to hold in place.

Next, using a double strand of yarn and a crochet hook, stitch the areas together to form the shoulder seams as indicated by the brackets in the Step 2 diagram.

Remove all clips.

Connect the left and right lower corners of the twisted Upper Back piece to the Lower Back at the underarm by weaving a few strands of yarn in and out.

Weave in the ends; cut the yarn.

WITH A CHUNKY YARN AND AN OPEN pattern, as in this design, I find it helpful to get an extra mile from the garment by securing the yarn ends after weaving them in using a sewing needle and matching thread to make a few tack stitches so they don't work their way out over time.

MAKE THE TIES

There are 4 double-strand ties on the front of the garment. Two of the ties are the remaining tail yarns from casting off the fronts. Trim these evenly to 12 in. after knotting the ends together.

To make the 2 additional ties, cut 2 single-strand lengths of yarn that are each 26 in.

long. Fold each strand in half. Push the yarn fold through the Front at the bust (or waist if preferred) using 1 strand on each front. You may want to try on the garment to find the best location for these ties.

Once the loop end is pushed through the stitch, slip both tails of the tie through the loop and pull to secure. It is like making one giant single piece of fringe (see p. 131). Use the other length to repeat. Knot the ends of each tie and trim to 12 in.

MULTISTRAND VARIEGATED ROVING YARN COWL

Sometimes I like a beginner project to teach a particular skill. This cowl teaches how to knit in the round using circular needles. The greatest advantage in using circular needles for a project such as a cowl is that there are no seams to stitch together when you're done—just a few tails to weave in. This project uses four strands of Super Bulky CYC 6 yarn held together to give the weight and heft of a Jumbo CYC 7 yarn. Jumbo CYC 7 is a new weight, and the size of the yarn is becoming more popular, but the color and style selection are limited. You'll find more options in CYC 5 Bulky and CYC 6 Super Bulky yarns. The four variegated strands also provide an appealing rustic color variation in the finished knit.

LEVEL
Beginner

YARN
4 skeins (a total of approximately 272 yd./ 249 m) variegated wool roving-type yarn, (CYC 6) Super Bulky

SHOWN IN
Isaac Mizrahi® Craft™ by Premier® Yarns; 85% acrylic, 15% wool; 68 yd. (62 m); 4 oz. (113 g); color: East End

NEEDLES & NOTIONS
1 pair U.S. size 50 (25 mm) circular knitting needles, 24 in. (60 cm) long

Stitch marker (made from a scrap of yarn as described on p. 31 and p. 130 or store-bought)

Crochet hook, size P/Q (15 mm) or similar size, to weave in the ends

GAUGE
Measured flat and stitched with 4 strands held together and worked as one in Stockinette Stitch:

4 stitches = 4 in.

6 rows = 4 in.

THE BIG PICTURE

I staggered the variegation of the 4 yarn strands to create a less striped, more muted effect once knitted. Also, due to the natural state of this yarn, the manufacturer states on the label that the yardage may vary. I suggest buying 1 additional skein, if possible, to ensure you have enough to complete your fabulous cowl.

FINISHED MEASUREMENTS

Cowl is 10 in. high when measured flat from cast-on edge to cast-off edge.

Total circumference is 36 in. along bottom edge.

MAKE THE COWL

Holding 4 strands of yarn together and working them as one, measure off 4 yd. Beginning with a slip knot as shown on pp. 14–15, cast on a total of 35 stitches using the Long-Tail Cast-On method shown on p. 14, leaving at least a 6-in. tail. Place a stitch marker on your needle after the last cast-on stitch. To make a stitch marker, I use a piece of contrasting yarn tied in a loop around the knitting needle, but you can purchase one as well; just make sure you buy one big enough to fit around your large needles.

You'll begin the first row by knitting into the first cast-on stitch, which will connect your work into a circle. Make sure the bottom edges of the cast-on stitches are all facing down and not twisted along any part of the needle (see p. 31). Knit all stitches around in a circle. When you come to the marker, just move it from the nonworking needle to the working needle. It marks the end of one row and the beginning of the next row.

ROWS 1-13: Knit across each row. Keep track of each completed row with a purchased stitch counter or by using a notepad and pen or pencil.

THERE ARE SEVERAL VARIETIES OF STITCH counters available. They all display the number of rows you've finished knitting. On some you turn a dial to advance the number; on others you click a button. In my opinion, a piece of paper and pen work just as well.

When working in a circle, you're always working on the right side. When you create the Stockinette Stitch using circular needles, you never have to purl any stitches. That's because you're never stitching on the wrong side, where purl stitches are typically worked.

Cast off as shown on pp. 21–22.

FINISHING

Weave in the cast-on and cast-off tails using a crochet hook as shown on p. 41.

DESIGNER'S BIG IDEA

Fringe can make a bold statement on any wearable including this cowl, and it's easy to make and add. I would only add fringe to the cast-on edge, and I would try to cut the variegation in a manner so that each fringe is one color, then stagger the color around. You will need an extra skein of yarn to add fringe, and if you want the fringe to be as even and neat as possible, cut it on a self-repairing cutting mat with a rotary cutter. I like to lay out the colors to decide on placement before I add them to the cowl.

TO MAKE FRINGE

Cut lengths of yarn about 14 in. long. Once cut, combine in groups of like colors of 4 strands, and fold one group of 4 strands in half (photo A).

Insert the folded end into a cast-on edge stitch (photo B), then pull the tails through the loop you have created at the folded end (photos C and D).

Snug the yarn to the edge of the garment, and voilà! One piece of fringe has been added. Continue in this manner all around until the remaining fringe is also inserted (photo E).

NOTE: The top of the fringe can "face" either way. It is a personal preference and depends on whether you pull the folded end of the fringe into the cast-on edge from the front of the stitch or the back.

A crochet hook can be helpful in pulling the folded yarn ends through the cast-on stitch, although some people prefer to simply poke the yarn through using a finger.

A

B

C

D

E

CONVERTIBLE BUTTON-ON COLLAR SCARF

I was playing around with the notion of adding or taking away pieces to make this scarf convertible, and I came up with the idea of buttoning on a separate piece. The big stitches that naturally occur when using size 50 needles allow for a buttonhole at any location without having to specifically knit one in, which offers more flexibility for a beginner. Here I chose to button on a collar piece, but you can get creative and try other ideas.

SKILL LEVEL
Beginner

YARN
Color A (solid): 1 skein (approximately 106 yd./97 m) acrylic/wool blend yarn, (CYC 6) Super Bulky

Color B (variegated): 3 to 4 skeins (a total of approximately 204 yd./187 m) acrylic/wool blend variegated yarn, (CYC 6) Super Bulky. (You actually need 2 full skeins and 2 half skeins of this yarn. I chose to use 4 skeins so I didn't have to divide the third skein in half, but if you are on a budget, you can divide the third skein in half, matching up color sections for the double strand requirement.)

SHOWN IN
Lion Brand Wool-Ease Thick & Quick; 80% acrylic, 20% wool; 106 yd. (97 m); 6 oz. (170 g); color: Pumpkin

Isaac Mizrahi Craft Sutton by Premier Yarns, 85% acrylic, 15% wool; (68 yd. (62 m); 4 oz. (113 g); color: Columbus

NEEDLES & NOTIONS
1 pair U.S. size 50 (25 mm) straight knitting needles, 14 in. (35.5 cm) long

Crochet hook, U.S. size Q (16 mm) or similar size, to weave in the ends

Five 1½-in.-wide buttons or any buttons that fit snugly through your stitches, depending on your finishing option.

Sewing needle and matching thread to sew on buttons

GAUGE

Measured flat in Garter Stitch using 3 strands of yarn:

5 stitches= 4 in.

7 rows= 4 in.

FINISHED MEASUREMENTS

Long Scarf Piece is 40 in. long by 7 in. wide, measured flat.

Short Collar Piece is 16 in. long by 7 in. wide, measured flat.

MAKE THE LONG SCARF PIECE

Holding 3 strands of yarn together from a prewound ball and working them as one, measure off 1¼ yd. Beginning with a slip knot as shown on pp. 14–15, cast on a total of 9 stitches using the Long-Tail Cast-On method shown on p. 14, leaving a 6-in. tail.

ROW 1 (WRONG SIDE OF WORK, WS): Knit across the row; turn your work.

ROW 2 (RIGHT SIDE OF WORK, RS): Knit across the row; turn your work.

These 2 rows create Garter Stitch, as shown on p. 23.

Repeat Rows 1 and 2 for a total of 64 rows.

Cast off as shown on pp. 21–22, leaving a 5-in. tail.

MAKE THE SHORT COLLAR PIECE

Holding 3 strands of yarn together from a prewound ball and working them as one, measure off 1¼ yd. Beginning with a slip knot as shown pp. 14–15, cast on a total of 9 stitches using the Long-Tail Cast-On method shown on p. 14, leaving a 6-in. tail.

Knit in Garter Stitch (knit every row) as with the Long Scarf Piece, for 28 rows.

Cast off as shown on pp. 21–22, leaving a 5-in. tail. Weave in all ends using a crochet hook as shown on p. 41.

THE BIG PICTURE

As you will see in the pattern instructions, I hold together 3 strands of yarn at the same time—1 solid and 2 variegated. I wanted to soften the variegation slightly to create a muted effect to the striping that occurs in the variegated yarn, so I used the solid yarn as a way to blend the yarns together. However, I took care to start at the same general color point on the 2 different skeins of variegated yarn so that the striping was not completely eliminated and the color changes of both strands came out in the same general area on the scarf.

Since each yarn contains a different yardage, I suggest prewinding the yarns into one big ball. This gives you the opportunity to attach each new yarn when a yarn runs out as you wind the ball instead of trying to do it while you are knitting. It also allows you to look at the variegation color striping when you start another skein to decide the best place along its colorway to tie on the new yarn.

ASSEMBLY

There are several ways to assemble the scarf. I chose to sew on buttons where noted so that the scarf can be unbuttoned and worn without the collar. Plus, the buttons add a nice touch! You can also fold the scarf as described and sew the buttons through all layers to permanently attach the collar if you want to pull this on over your head when you wear it. Or, you can permanently sew both pieces together as instructed and eliminate the buttons entirely.

Here's how to assemble the pieces using functioning buttons:

STEP 1: Attach Buttons 1 and 2 to the inside corners of the Long Scarf Piece (photo A).

STEP 2: Sew 3 buttons (Buttons 3, 4, and 5) equally spaced from the center out on the Short Collar Piece, approximately 1 in. up from the lower edge (photo B).

STEP 3: Place the Short Scarf Piece on a flat surface, and place the Long Scarf Piece on top, overlapping 1 in. as shown (photo C). The long edges run horizontally. Button the Short Collar Piece onto the Long Scarf Piece, positioning Button 4 between the 40th and

the 42nd row from the cast-on edge of the Long Piece (photo D). Flip over onto the flat surface. Buttons 1 and 2 should be on the top edge of the long scarf.

STEP 4: Fold over the short side of the scarf as shown in photo E. Then fold over the long side of the scarf as shown in photo F, placing Button 1 through a stitch on row 21. The button should be centered in row 21 of the scarf piece.

STEP 5: Pull Buttons 3 and 5 from the Short Collar Piece through the Long Scarf Piece that has been crisscrossed, going through all layers of the Long Scarf Piece and making sure to align them in a row with Button 1 (photo F). Flip the scarf back over so that Button 4 is on the center back as shown in photo G.

STEP 6: Button the remaining end button (Button 2) through the center back of the Short Collar Piece as shown in photo H, taking care to align the buttons vertically.

The scarf is ready to pull over your head (photo I). Whichever way you choose, this collar creates big drama on the back of the neck. (You may want to wear your hair up if it is long to show off the collar.)

Long Scarf Piece

Button 1   Button 2   **A**

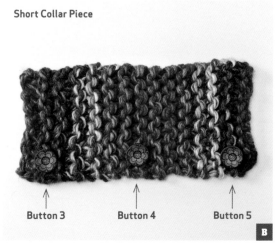

Short Collar Piece

Button 3   Button 4   Button 5   **B**

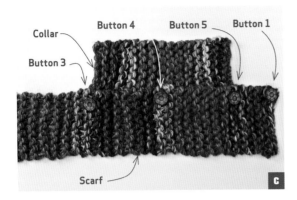

Collar

Button 3

Button 4

Button 5

Button 1

Scarf

C

D

Flip the connected pieces over and fold over the short side then the long side.

Fold.

Button 5

Button 1

E

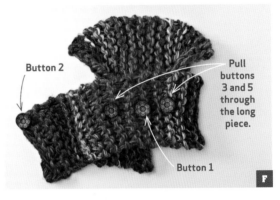

Button 2

Pull buttons 3 and 5 through the long piece.

Button 1

F

Flip scarf over. Button 4 is on the center back.

Button 2

G

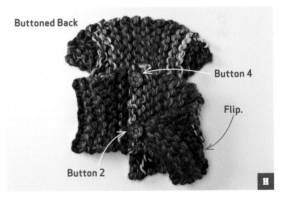

Buttoned Back

Button 4

Flip.

Button 2

H

Buttoned Front

Scarf is ready to be pulled over your head.

I

MULTISTRAND PULLOVER
KERCHIEF
WITH
POM-POMS

Even if you're a beginner, you can create a statement piece. This project is a case in point. It uses a simple knitting stitch—Stockinette Stitch (one every knitter should know how to make)—and a simple shape—a square—and combines them to make a fun, unique accessory. You'll feel and look like a million bucks knowing the project was simple and the results are spectacular!

SKILL LEVEL
Beginner

YARN
Color A: 2 skeins (a total of approximately 128 yd./117 m) novelty eyelash yarn (CYC 5), Bulky

Color B: 2 skeins (a total of approximately 162 yd./148 m) acrylic yarn (CYC 6), Super Bulky

Color C: 2 skeins (a total of approximately 162 yd./148 m) acrylic yarn (CYC 6), Super Bulky

Color D: 2 skeins (a total of approximately 200 yd./183 m) novelty chenille yarn (CYC 5), Bulky

SHOWN IN
Color A: Lion Brand Fun Fur; 100% polyester; 64 yd. (58 m); 1.75 oz. (50 g); color: Neon Lime

Color B: Lion Brand Hometown USA; 100% acrylic; 81 yd. (74 m); 5 oz. (142 g); color: Monterey Lime

Color C: Lion Brand Hometown USA; 100% acrylic; 81 yd. (74 m); 5 oz. (142 g); color: Key Lime

Color D: Lion Brand Chenille; 75% acrylic, 18% polyester, 7% nylon; 100 yd. (91 m); 2.5 oz. (71 g); color: Emerald

NOTE: The skeins for this project are used to make both the kerchief and the two pom-poms included in the instructions. Purchase only 1 skein of each yarn if you prefer not to use pom-poms or, alternatively, attach premade pom-poms such as Lion Brand The Pom.

NEEDLES & NOTIONS

1 pair U.S. size 50 (25 mm) straight knitting
needles, 14 in. (35.5 cm) long

3⅜-in. (85 mm) pom-pom maker, such as
Clover Large Pom-Pom maker (or size of
your choice), or 2 purchased pom-poms,
such as Lion Brand The Pom.

Crochet hook, size Q (16 mm) or similar size
to weave in the ends

Sewing needle and matching heavy sewing
thread, such as button thread

GAUGE

Measured flat using multistrand yarn in
Stockinette Stitch

3 stitches = 4 in.

6 rows = 4 in.

FINISHED MEASUREMENTS

Kerchief is 20 in. wide, measured flat across
the cast-on edge.

Kerchief is 18 in. long, measured along the
side edge.

SOMETIMES KNITTING WITH MULTIPLE
strands of yarn can be frustrating because the
yarns may twist as you work and may affect the
gauge and overall texture of the knitted piece.
To compensate for the twist, gently untwist the
yarn by rotating the balls in the opposite direction periodically, which will help keep them from
getting tangled. The other option is to prewind
the yarns together into one big ball.

NOTE: You should double-check your gauge
before making the kerchief by knitting a
swatch (see p. 42) to make sure you achieve
the recommended gauge measurements.
With a simple project like this one, it's
usually fine if the gauge is a little off. For
this project, just make sure you can fit your
head through the opening after folding the

DESIGNER'S BIG IDEA

If your budget allows, make 2 squares and
wear one on each side of your neck like a
giant collar. Place the 2 squares on a flat
surface and position them as diamonds.
Overlap one diamond over the other by
a third of the total distance across the
diamond so that you will be able to connect
the two shapes. Just weave a length of
multistrand yarn through the center of the
overlapped areas to connect the 2 pieces.
Attach the pom-poms to the cast-on and
cast-off strands as with the single square
project, and fold the attached diamonds in
half as before, with the pom-poms opposite
the fold. Tie the pom-pom tails to secure
around your neck. Make each square the
same color, or knit them in complementary
or contrasting colors for a totally different
look. Embrace the opportunity to get
creative with this simple pattern and have
fun expressing yourself!

square into a triangle, but before connecting
it. If you've chosen to use different yarn
combinations than what I've called for
and your gauge is too tight, knit a few
extra rows or add a few extra stitches in
each row to compensate for the difference
in measurements.

MAKE THE KERCHIEF

Holding 4 strands of yarn (1 from each color)
together and working them as one, measure
off 2 yd. Beginning with a slip knot as shown
on pp. 14–15, cast on a total of 18 stitches
using the Long-Tail Cast-On method shown
on p. 14, leaving a 1-yd. tail to use later.

ROW 1 (RIGHT SIDE OF WORKS, RS): Knit across the row.

ROW 2 (WRONG SIDE OF WORKS, WS): Purl across the row.

Rows 1 and 2 make up a basic knit pattern called Stockinette Stitch as shown on p. 23. Continue to work in Stockinette Stitch by repeating Rows 1 and 2 for a total of 28 rows, keeping track of your rows with a stitch counter or notepad and pen.

Cast off as shown on pp. 21–22, taking care to cast off on the right side of the work so that the cast-on and cast-off tails end up on opposite corners of the finished square. Be sure to leave a 1-yd. tail to use later to attach to the pom-pom. (See p. 142 for making the pom-pom.)

FINISH THE KERCHIEF

Position the finished piece on a flat surface in a diamond shape (see drawing A below).

The pom-pom tails should be opposite each other at the top and bottom of the diamond.

Fold the diamond in half by bringing the top of the diamond down to meet the bottom of the diamond (see drawing B at right).

Attach the 2 corners of the folded edge together (points 1 and 2 in the drawing)

to form the scarf's neck opening (these corners have no tails); see drawing C below. Using sewing thread or 1 strand of acrylic yarn, stitch the 2 points securely together and tie off. Weave in the ends as shown on p. 41 and trim the excess.

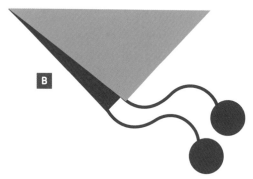

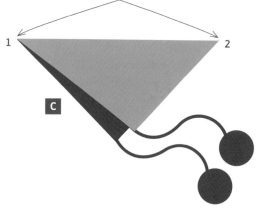

Connect point 1 to point 2 to form neck opening.

Place on flat surface in diamond shape and fold top half down.

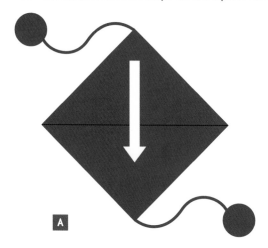

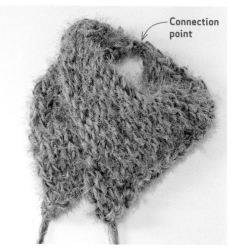

Connection point

DESIGNER'S BIG IDEA

The pom-pom tails add a fun touch to this knit top, and making them is easy. Follow the directions below.

TO MAKE POM-POMS

Tape the beginning and ends of the yarn tails to a piece of 1¾-in.-wide cardboard, then wrap the yarn around it. I wrapped all 4 yarns around 20 times (photo A).

Cut the yarn down the center of the cardboard to get the right size of cut yarn pieces (photo B).

Next, make a little stack of cut yarn strands. Before tying them together in the center to form the pom-pom, insert the end of the cast-on (or cast-off) tails into the stack as if they were part of the pom-pom. The pom-pom should be positioned about 10 in. down the tail.

Next, use heavy sewing thread to tie the yarn strands into a pom-pom (photo C). I have found the sewing thread to be helpful in creating a very tight center, which holds the cut yarn strands more securely. Yarn can stretch a little when pulled tightly, so if you used yarn instead of heavy sewing thread, it might loosen with time (heavy sewing thread is less likely to do so). Then I hid the sewing thread by tying off the pom-pom with matching multistrand yarns on top of the thread.

Reinforce the kerchief yarn tails with button thread and a sewing needle by tacking the

tails to the center of the pom-pom so they can't slip out.

Make a second pom-pom at the end of the cast-off tail. Trim the pom-pom yarns to make them even, and trim the tail so it is the same length as the pom-pom yarns (photo D).

You can also use a pom-pom maker to make pom-poms, but before assembling the pom-pom, **do this additional step:** Insert the tail yarns into the center of the cut yarn stack before tying the pom-pom together. When using a purchased pom-pom maker, I hold 4 strands of yarn together and wrap them 20 times around each section.

PULL-THROUGH
TEXTURED
RUSTIC
WRAP

Handcrafting is back! Some people are gravitating toward this creative pastime as a backlash against technology, and others love the idea of making something truly unique. This wrap takes the idea one step further thanks to the yarn, which looks "homespun." Through the use of a thick-and-thin spinning technique, this yarn reminds us of a time when all yarns were made on a spinning wheel. I have taken a historic, nostalgic-looking yarn and made it look contemporary through the use of a modern silhouette.

SKILL LEVEL
Advanced

YARN
4 skeins (a total of approximately 368 yd./ 336 m) wool/acrylic blend novelty slub-type yarn, (CYC 6) Super Bulky

NOTE: Due to yardage variations in chunky acrylic yarns, I suggest buying an extra skein to ensure you'll have enough yarn in the same dye lot. Most stores permit you to return an unused yarn skein within a reasonable length of time, provided you have the receipt.

SHOWN IN
Buttercream™ Luxe Craft Thick & Thin; 52% wool, 48% acrylic; 92 yd. (84 m), 5 oz. (140 g); color: Cream

NEEDLES & NOTIONS
1 pair U.S. size 50 (25 mm) straight knitting needles, 24 in. (60 cm) long
Crochet hook, U.S. size K or 10½ (6.5 mm) used to make the cable and connect the pieces. (A large stitch holder or cable hook can be substituted to make cables.)

GAUGE
Measured flat in Stockinette Stitch using 2 strands of yarn:
4 stitches = 4 in.
6 rows = 4 in.

FINISHED MEASUREMENTS

Hem is 66 in. measured flat along the entire hem including the cable portion (refer to photo A on p. 148 for hem area).

Neckline is 50 in. measured flat along the entire neckline including cable portion (refer to photo A on p. 148 for neckline area).

Wrap is 14 in. long measured flat at the short row angled edge.

CABLE PATTERNS

C16F: Slide the first 8 stitches onto the crochet hook (or cable hook) and hold at the FRONT of the work. Knit across the next 8 stitches on the nonworking needle in the same row. Slide the stitches from the crochet hook back onto the nonworking needle, taking care not to twist the stitches. Knit the 8 stitches just placed back on the nonworking needle.

C16B: Slide the first 8 stitches onto the crochet hook (or cable hook) and hold at the BACK of the work. Knit across the next 8 stitches on the nonworking needle in the same row. Slide the stitches from the crochet hook back onto the nonworking needle, taking care not to twist the stitches. Knit the 8 stitches just placed back on the nonworking needle.

MAKE THE WRAP

Holding 2 strands of yarn together and working them as one jumbo yarn, measure off 2 yd. Beginning with a slip knot as shown on pp. 14–15, cast on a total of 16 stitches using the Long-Tail Cast-On method shown on p. 14. The leftover yarn tail will be woven in later. If it gets in the way, loosely wind and knot it.

ROW 1 (WRONG SIDE OF WORK, WS): Purl across the row. Turn your work.

ROW 2 (RIGHT SIDE OF WORK, RS): Knit across the row. Turn your work.

THE BIG PICTURE

The thick and thin areas of the yarn create "slubs" where the yarn is less twisted and therefore puffs out in random places. In this project, the texture is slightly modified by using 2 yarn strands together, which form a jumbo yarn size worked on the largest size needles. Working the 2 yarn strands together makes the surface of the knit slightly more uniform and also helps with stability and drape once made into a knitted garment. Two other techniques are employed in this wrap. One jumbo cable forward and one jumbo cable backward at opposite ends of the knitted piece create a twisted area as well as holes in which to pull the back end of the wrap through the front, creating a dramatic closure. Additionally, the use of "short rows" is a technique for fitting knitted garments around body curves. In this pattern, they are used to "turn the corner" around the shoulder, making one side of the piece more curved than the other, thus creating a shorter edge for the neckline and a longer edge for the hemline.

ROW 3 (WS): Repeat Row 1.
ROW 4 (RS): Repeat Row 2.
ROW 5 (WS): Repeat Row 1.
ROW 6 (RS): Repeat Row 2.
ROW 7 (WS): Repeat Row 1

BEGIN CABLE ROW

ROW 8 (RS): C16F, as described above. (Make sure you don't twist the stitches when you put them back on the nonworking needle.)

ROW 9 (WS): Purl across the row.

ROWS 10–29: Continue knitting in Stockinette Stitch as shown on p. 23, where all stitches on the wrong side of the work are purled and all stitches on the right side of the work are knit.

BEGIN SHORT ROWS

ROW 30 (RS): Knit 14; turn your work without knitting the remaining 2 stitches.

ROW 31 (WS): Slip the first stitch without purling. Purl 13; turn your work.

ROW 32 (RS): Knit 12; turn your work without knitting the remaining 4 stitches.

ROW 33 (WS): Slip the first stitch without purling. Purl 11; turn your work.

ROW 34 (RS): Knit 10; turn your work without knitting the remaining 6 stitches.

ROW 35 (WS): Slip the first stitch without purling. Purl 9; turn your work.

ROW 36 (RS): Knit 8; turn your work without knitting the remaining 8 stitches.

ROW 37 (WS): Slip the first stitch without purling. Purl 7; turn your work.

ROW 38 (RS): Knit 6; turn your work without knitting the remaining 10 stitches.

ROW 39 (WS): Slip the first stitch without purling. Purl 5; turn your work.

ROW 40 (RS): Knit 4; turn your work without knitting the remaining 12 stitches.

ROW 41 (WS): Slip the first stitch without purling. Purl 3; turn your work.

ROW 42 (RS): Knit 2; turn your work without knitting the remaining 14 stitches.

ROW 43 (WS): Slip the first stitch without purling. Purl 1; turn your work.

ROW 44 (RS): Knit across the row; turn your work.

ROW 45 (WS): Purl across the row; turn your work.

COMPLETE SHORT ROWS

ROW 46 (RS): Knit 14; turn your work without knitting the remaining 2 stitches.

ROW 47 (WS): Slip the first stitch without purling. Purl 13; turn your work.

ROW 48 (RS): Knit 12; turn your work without knitting the remaining 4 stitches.

ROW 49 (WS): Slip the first stitch without purling. Purl 11; turn your work.

ROW 50 (RS): Knit 10; turn your work without knitting the remaining 6 stitches.

ROW 51 (WS): Slip the first stitch without purling. Purl 9; turn your work.

ROW 52 (RS): Knit 8; turn your work without knitting the remaining 8 stitches.

ROW 53 (WS): Slip the first stitch without purling. Purl 7; turn your work.

ROW 54 (RS): Knit 6; turn your work without knitting the remaining 10 stitches.

ROW 55 (WS): Slip the first stitch without purling. Purl 5; turn your work.

ROW 56 (RS): Knit 4; turn your work without knitting the remaining 12 stitches.

ROW 57 (WS): Slip the first stitch without purling. Purl 3; turn your work.

ROW 58 (RS): Knit 2; turn your work without knitting the remaining 14 stitches.

ROW 59 (WS): Slip the first stitch without purling. Purl 1; turn your work.

ROW 60 (RS): Knit across the row.

ROW 61 (WS): Purl across the row.

ROWS 62–81: Continue knitting in Stockinette Stitch as shown on p. 23, where all stitches on the wrong side of your work are purled and all stitches on the right side of your work are knit.

BEGIN CABLE ROW

ROW 82 (RS): C16B, as shown in the instructions on the facing page. (Make sure you don't twist the stitches when you put them back on the nonworking needle.) Turn your work.

ROW 83 (WS): Purl across the row.

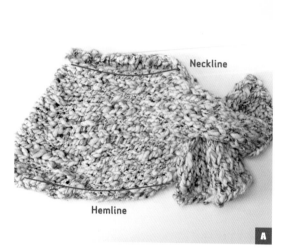

Neckline

Hemline

A

Pull.

Hole created by cable

B

C

D

ROWS 84–89: Continue knitting in Stockinette Stitch.

ROW 90 (RS): Cast off as shown on pp. 21–22, leaving a 6-in. tail.

FINISHING

CREATE THE SHOULDER AND NECK OPENING:

On a flat surface, place the garment folded in half as shown in photo A. Using 1 strand of yarn approximately 12 in. long and the crochet hook, weave the yarn back and forth as shown on p. 34 for 5 rows, leaving a neck opening of 20 in. This shoulder seam will secure the wrap so that it stays put on the body. Take care to align the rows (see the red arrow in photo B). Weave in the ends and trim the yarn, taking care not to cut the work.

Place the cast-off edge of the knitted piece through the opening made in the cable front technique (photo C). Pull until the cable back twist aligns with the cable front twist as shown in photo D. Add a small tack under the cable if desired to keep the twist in place.

DOLMAN SLEEVE CHUNKY TOP

Once upon a time, if you knit anything that was super wide or had a hole in it, that was considered a mistake. I have always been one of those girls who calls things like that "happy accidents," and now it is called FASHION! This garment has a dolman (or batwing) look that is very modern right now in the fashion world. It is almost a cross between a poncho and a sweater. I offer a variation that pushes the silhouette even further with a peek-a-boo shoulder, where part of the shoulder seam is intentionally not connected so the tips of your shoulders peek through. Since it is very cold where I live, I chose to sew the entire shoulder seam closed. But you can go ahead with the open seam variation and take a cue from the runway by layering a thin knit under this chunky one. Either way, you will have style for miles!

SKILL LEVEL
Advanced

YARN
8 skeins (a total of approximately 360 yd./ 330 m) acrylic/wool blend yarn, (CYC 7) Jumbo

SHOWN IN
Red Heart Grande Metallic™; 79% acrylic, 20% wool, 1% metallic; 45 yd. (41 m); 5.29 oz. (150 g); color: Smoke

NEEDLES & NOTIONS
1 pair U.S. size 19 (15 mm) straight knitting needles, 14 in. (35.5 cm) long, for the rib portions of the pattern

1 pair U.S. size 50 (25 mm) straight knitting needles, 14 in. (35.5 cm) long, for the main body of the pattern

Crochet hook, U.S. size Q (16 mm) to make cables

NOTE: A cable needle or cable hook can be used to make the cable if preferred, but they are hard to find in jumbo size.

Crochet hook, U.S. size K or 10½ (6.5 mm), for finishing

GAUGE FOR RIB PORTIONS
Measured in 1 x 1 Rib Stitch with size 19 needles:

8 stitches = 4 in.

10 rows = 4 in.

GAUGE FOR MAIN BODY

Measured in Garter Stitch with size 50 needles:

5 stitches = 4 in.

6 rows = 4 in.

FINISHED MEASUREMENTS

Front and Back are 24 in. wide, measured flat across the bottom of the Rib Stitch.

Center Front and Center Back are 24 in. long, measured flat from the top of the neck piece to the bottom hem.

Front is 32 in. wide, measured flat across at the widest part of the dolman section.

Neck opening circumference is 26 in. at the top of the cast-off rib.

REVIEW THE FOLLOWING TECHNIQUES before starting. I always read through a pattern before I start a new project to make sure I am familiar with all of the techniques used. For example, this pattern requires you to know Make One Front and Back (M1FB), Cable Forward (CXF where "X" defines the number of stitches making up the cable), changing needle sizes, Knit Two Together (K2TOG), and Slip, Slip, Knit (SSK). Learn more about these in the Basics section, starting on p. 8.

CABLE PATTERN

This pattern requires a **C7F,** or **Cable 7 Forward**. Here is how I made the C7F using the large crochet hook:

Slide 3 stitches from the nonworking needle to the crochet hook (these are the first 3 stitches from the C7F), and hold the crochet hook in the FRONT of the work. Start using the working needle to knit the next 4 stitches from the nonworking needle. You will see that as you begin these 4 stitches, you will knit across the purl

THE BIG PICTURE

Purl stitch

This top requires you to make a cable. Most often a cable needle or cable hook is used. Super-large cable needles and hooks can be difficult to find, so I used a large crochet hook to cable this top instead. It worked like a dream because the yarn didn't slip off. Use whichever tool works best for you. Most cables are created over an even number of stitches. This one is created over 7 stitches with a purl stitch in the center so that it ends up centered on the ribbing at the neck. It produces a slightly different cable, which works beautifully in this garment.

stitch; don't worry—I promise it will be fine! Slide the initial 3 stitches back onto the nonworking needle in order, taking care not to twist them when putting them back on. Once all the stitches are back on the nonworking needle, set the crochet hook aside, and knit the 3 remaining stitches in the C7F pattern. You have now completed a C7F.

JUST REMEMBER THAT ON THE BACK OF the work on the row after you have made the cable, you will be putting a knit stitch (purl stitch on the right side) back in the center of the C7F. It is explained in the pattern.

MAKE THE FRONT

Using 1 strand of yarn and size 19 needles, measure off 2½ yd. Beginning with a slip knot as shown on pp. 14–15, cast on a total of 43 stitches using the Long-Tail Cast-On method shown on p. 14, leaving a 1-yd. tail for use later.

Begin the Rib Stitch as follows (see p. 24):

ROW 1 (WRONG SIDE OF WORK, WS): *Purl 1, Knit 1 (P1, K1)*; repeat from * to * across. Purl the last stitch. This is the first row of Rib Stitch. Turn your work.

ROW 2 (RIGHT SIDE OF WORK, RS): *Knit 1, Purl 1 (K1, P1)*; repeat from * to * across. Knit the last stitch. This is the second row of Rib Stitch. Turn your work.

ROW 3 (WS): *P1, K1*; repeat from * to * across. Purl the last stitch.

ROW 4 (RS): *K1, P1*; repeat from * to * across. Knit the last stitch.

ROW 5 (WS): *P1, K1*; repeat from * to * across. Purl the last stitch.

Switch to size 50 needles by using the working needle in the new size and knitting off the size 19 needles.

ROW 6 (RS): With the size 50 working needle, Knit 17, Purl 1, Knit 3, Purl 1, Knit 3, Purl 1, Knit 17. You should have 43 stitches.

ROW 7 (WS): Using both size 50 needles, Purl 17, Knit 1, Purl 3, Knit 1, Purl 3, Knit 1, Purl 17.

ROW 8 (RS): Knit 17, Purl 1, Knit 3, Purl 1, Knit 3, Purl 1, Knit 17.

ROW 9 (WS): Purl 17, Knit 1, Purl 3, Knit 1, Purl 3, Knit 1, Purl 17.

ROW 10 (RS) (CABLE ROW): Knit 17, Purl 1, C7F, Purl 1, Knit 17.

ROW 11 (WS): Purl 17, Knit 1, Purl 3, Knit 1, Purl 3, Knit 1, Purl 17.

ROW 12 (RS): Knit 17, Purl 1, Knit 3, Purl 1, Knit 3, Purl 1, Knit 17.

Repeat Rows 11 and 12 until the end of Row 15.

ROW 16 (RS) (CABLE ROW): Knit 17, Purl 1, C7F, Purl 1, Knit 17.

ROW 17 (WS): Purl 17, Knit 1, Purl 3, Knit 1, Purl 3, Knit 1, Purl 17.

ROW 18 (RS): Make One Front and Back (M1FB) as shown on p. 29, Knit 16, Purl 1, Knit 3, Purl 1, Knit 3, Purl 1, Knit 16, M1FB. You should have 45 stitches.

ROW 19 (WS): Purl 18, Knit 1, Purl 3, Knit 1, Purl 3, Knit 1, Purl 18.

ROW 20 (RS): M1FB, Knit 17, Purl 1, Knit 3, Purl 1, Knit 3, Purl 1, Knit 17, M1FB. You should have 47 stitches.

ROW 21 (WS): Purl 19, Knit 1, Purl 3, Knit 1, Purl 3, Knit 1, Purl 19.

ROW 22 (RS) (CABLE ROW): M1FB, Knit 18, Purl 1, C7F, Purl 1, Knit 18, M1FB. You should have 49 stitches.

ROW 23 (WS): Purl 20, Knit 1, Purl 3, Knit 1, Purl 3, Knit 1, Purl 20.

ROW 24 (RS): Knit 20, Purl 1, Knit 3, Purl 1, Knit 3, Purl 1, Knit 20.

Repeat Rows 23 and 24 until the end of Row 27.

ROW 28 (RS) (CABLE ROW): Knit 20, Purl 1, C7F, Purl 1, Knit 20.

ROW 29 (WS): Purl 20, Knit 1, Purl 3, Knit 1, Purl 3, Knit 1, Purl 20.

ROW 30 (RS): Cast off 5 stitches as shown on pp. 21–22. Knit 14, Purl 1, Knit 3, Purl 1, Knit 3, Purl 1, Knit 20. You should have 44 stitches.

ROW 31 (WS): Cast off 5 stitches WHILE PURLING as shown on pp. 21–22. Purl 14,

Knit 1, Purl 3, Knit 1, Purl 3, Knit 1, Purl 15. You should have 39 stitches.

ROW 32 (RS): Cast off 5 stitches. Knit 9, Purl 1, Knit 3, Purl 1, Knit 3, Purl 1, Knit 15. You should have 34 stitches.

ROW 33 (WS): Cast off 5 stitches WHILE PURLING. Purl 9, Knit 1, Purl 3, Knit 1, Purl 3, Knit 1, Purl 10. You should have 29 stitches.

ROW 34 (RS) (CABLE ROW): Cast off 5 stitches. Knit 4, Purl 1, C7F, Purl 1, Knit 10. You should have 24 stitches.

ROW 35 (WS): Cast off 5 stitches WHILE PURLING. Purl 4, Knit 1, Purl 3, Knit 1, Purl 3, Knit 1, Purl 5. You should have 19 stitches.

Switch to size 19 needle for the working needle for Row 36.

ROW 36 (RS): With the size 19 working needle, *K1, P1*; repeat from * to * across. Knit the last stitch.

ROW 37 (WS): Using both size 19 needles, *P1, K1*; repeat from * to * across. Purl the last stitch.

ROW 38 (RS): *K1, P1*; repeat from * to * across. Knit the last stitch.

ROW 39 (WS): *P1, K1*; repeat from * to * across. Purl the last stitch.

ROW 40 (RS): Cast off all stitches in Rib Stitch, leaving a 2-yd. tail.

MAKE THE BACK

Make the Back in the same way as the Front.

FINISHING

Place the Front and Back pieces on a flat surface with wrong sides together. Using the size K hook and the cast-off tail, work your way down the ribbed neck on each side, weaving the tail back and forth to connect the sides of the neck as shown on p. 34.

Once you have finished weaving the neck together, switch to the mock-grafting method shown on p. 35. Begin connecting the cast-off areas on the shoulders until you reach the end of the shoulder. Weave in the tail and cut any excess. For the peek-a-boo variation mentioned in the beginning of the pattern, you can connect the collar and weave in the tails, then instead of sewing up the shoulder seams, place a few strategic mock grafting stitches at each of the "steps" found along the edge of the shoulder to create a peek-a-boo look. Weave in the ends as shown on p. 41 and cut any excess.

CONNECT THE SIDES

Starting at the bottom of the sides, using 1 strand of yarn approximately 2 yd. long, weave the yarn back and forth on the side seams to connect the pieces until you reach the end of the angled dolman area, leaving an opening for the armhole in the straight section of the work. Cut the excess yarn to 6 in. and weave in the end.

METRIC EQUIVALENCY CHART

One inch equals approximately 2.54 centimeters. To convert inches to centimeters, multiply the figure in inches by 2.54 and round off to the nearest half centimeter, or use the chart below, whose figures are rounded off (1 centimeter equals 10 millimeters).

⅛ in. = 3 mm		9 in. = 23 cm
¼ in. = 6 mm		10 in. = 25.5 cm
⅜ in. = 1 cm		12 in. = 30.5 cm
½ in. = 1.3 cm		14 in. = 35.5 cm
⅝ in. = 1.5 cm		15 in. = 38 cm
¾ in. = 2 cm		16 in. = 40.5 cm
⅞ in. = 2.2 cm		18 in. = 45.5 cm
1 in. = 2.5 cm		20 in. = 51 cm
2 in. = 5 cm		21 in. = 53.5 cm
3 in. = 7.5 cm		22 in. = 56 cm
4 in. = 10 cm		24 in. = 61 cm
5 in. = 12.5 cm		25 in. = 63.5 cm
6 in. = 15 cm		36 in. = 92 cm
7 in. = 18 cm		45 in. = 114.5 cm
8 in. = 20.5 cm		60 in. = 152 cm

INDEX